Christmas 2002

For: _Karin & Dean_

From: _Sharon & Steve_

Everywhere—everywhere, Christmas tonight!
Christmas in lands of the fir tree and pine,
Christmas in lands of the palm tree and vine,
Christmas where snow peaks stand solemn and
   white,
Christmas where cornfields lie sunny and
   bright,
Everywhere—everywhere, Christmas tonight!

PHILLIPS BROOKS

3001 Things We Love About Christmas

Copyright 2000 by The Zondervan Corporation

ISBN 0-310-97869-6

Requests for information should be addressed to:

■ ZondervanPublishingHouse
Grand Rapids, Michigan 49530
http://www.zondervan.com

Project Editor: Pat Matuszak
Associate Editor: Molly Detweiler
Cover Design: Jager and Associates
Interior Design: Laura Blost
Text Design: Robert Monacelli

Printed in the United States of America

00 01 02/RRD/ 4 3 2 1

3001 THINGS WE LOVE ABOUT CHRISTMAS

Zondervan Gifts

We have a gift for inspiration™

* leather gloves with fur liners
* linen aprons with Christmas decorations: puff paint, embroidery, cross stitching, appliqué, or "Kiss the Cook!" lettering
* little kid elves with plastic pointy ears
* snowplows
* Granny and Granddad's house
* a white velvet bridal gown
* Christmas window clings
* red poinsettias around the sanctuary
* antique baby spoons and cups
* "'leven pipers piping"
* "A mysterious money order for $350 in your doorway the year when you don't know how you will buy your children's gifts."
* "angels bending near the earth to touch their harps of gold"
* baby all wrapped up in a quilt
* "Christmas gives me the opportunity to show the light of Christ to all I come in contact with."
* little girls with black patent leather shoes and lacy white anklet socks
* going to the attic with Grandpa to bring down the decorations
* after-ski boots
* snowmen made from marshmallows
* "Come on over!"
* red cardinals eating berries outside the window

O COME, O COME EMMANUEL

O come, O come, Emmanuel,
And ransom captive Israel,
That mourns in lonely exile here
Until the Son of God appear.
Rejoice! Rejoice!
Emmanuel shall come to thee, O Israel.

O come, Thou Day-spring, come and cheer
Our spirits by Thine advent here;
Disperse the gloomy clouds of night,
And death's dark shadows put to flight.
Rejoice! Rejoice!
Emmanuel shall come to thee, O Israel.

O come, Desire of nations, bind
In one the hearts of all mankind;
Bid Thou our sad divisions cease,
And be Thyself our King of Peace.
Rejoice! Rejoice!
Emmanuel shall come to thee, O Israel.

TRANSLATED BY JOHN MASON NEALE

❋ "Christmas is the only day of the year each person searches for the love of Christ in each other; therefore they finally see it."

❋ the ski shop: Thinsulate everything, packet hand warmers, Fanny Packs and fur-lined after-ski boots

❋ a pinto pony wading through snow

❋ "Footprints in the Sand" in a frame

❋ baby Jesus born in a barn

❋ "I like to look at the stars and wonder what the star of Bethlehem must have looked like to the wise men."

❋ "Les anges dans nos campagnes . . ."

❋ quilted aprons with ruffles

❋ snowflake stars

❋ Christmas windows in department stores

❋ "let us all with one accord sing praises to our heavenly Lord"

❋ almond butter

❋ "Looking through the family album with my wife and remembering the happy years together."

❋ my grandpa and uncles trying to top each other's gag gifts each year

❋ passing a candle around the dinner table while each person tells how Christ has been their light during the past year

❋ being the giver of a gift that is so good it brings tears to the eyes of the receiver

The universal joy of Christmas is certainly wonderful. We ring the bells when princes are born, or toll a mournful dirge when great men pass away. Nations have their red-letter days, their carnivals and festivals, but once a year and only once, the whole world stands still to celebrate the advent of a life. Only Jesus of Nazareth claims this worldwide, undying remembrance. You cannot cut Christmas out of the calendar, nor out of the heart of the world.

ANONYMOUS

I like Christmas because it's the one time of the year when people celebrate the birth of Jesus and submit to a spirit of thanksgiving, kindness, giving, and love. Many relationships are restored during that time of the year, and people don't even realize that it is the Spirit of Christ Jesus at work in their hearts.

NEIL HUTTON

Christmas Pageants

* little faces peeking out from behind the stage curtain
* the director calling, "Places everyone!" at the Christmas play
* homemade animal costumes
* nervous first-time actors
* proud parents watching the play
* "I get to be a sheep!"
* kids dressed like angels
* kids dressed like angels, fighting
* little kids dressed like doves trying to "coo"
* two kids dressed like two halves of the cow
* a child actor trying to walk and sing like a camel
* the wise men's crowns tipping
* heavy velvet stage curtains
* theater spotlights
* the swish of the children's choir robes
* little boys who love to ad lib
* snowflake toddlers holding hands as they come onstage
* everyone coming out for a bow at the end
* applause, applause, applause

* babies with pacifiers
* "Oh, you shouldn't have!"
* an Olan Mills family portrait
* a crayon family portrait
* "on the first day of Christmas, my true love gave to me"
* "Passing out presents as my dad's 'helper' when he played Santa at the department store."
* "peace on earth, good will to men"
* cinnamon pecans
* the ski rental room
* God's promise to King David
* an angel hovering over the stable
* "People take it better when you play tricks on them or surprise them at Christmas."
* "shepherds watch are keeping"
* red brick storefronts
* baby napping in a travel carrier
* a pony ride
* snow-brick molds
* "Silent Night! Holy Night!"
* cinnamon raisin bread
* "that glorious song of old"
* Christmas cards that people write letters in instead of just signing their names
* gift bags with foil stars on them

Christmas is the season for kindling the fire of hospitality in the hall, the genial flame of charity in the heart.

WASHINGTON IRVING

I know not how that Bethlehem's Babe
    Could in the Godhead be;
I only know the Manger Child
    Has brought God's life to me.

HARRY WEBB FARRINGTON

The joy of brightening other lives, bearing each others' burdens, easing others' loads and supplanting empty hearts and lives with generous gifts becomes for us the magic of Christmas.

W. C. JONES

❄ how Grandma keeps warning, "No more candy canes; you'll spoil your appetite."

❄ how Grandpa keeps saying, "This is the last one" when he gives out more candy

❄ "The sweet sounds of a choir reminding us of the light and joy Jesus brings to our lives."

❄ "twelve drummers drumming"

❄ reservations at a fancy restaurant

❄ going to a restaurant that doesn't need reservations

❄ a Christmas Eve together with my whole family

❄ a puppy snuggling with a little boy

❄ gold candelabra

❄ "We'd love to have you stay with us!"

❄ "what child is this, who, laid to rest on Mary's lap, is sleeping?"

❄ "God gave his only Son!"

❄ cloves

❄ babies who bang spoons on their high chair trays

❄ God's promise to Abraham about the stars and the Savior to come

❄ the silver star that led the way to Bethlehem

The Sights and Sounds of the Season

* cream "clouds" swirling in coffee
* the whish of big black umbrellas opening
* a shoveled path
* a church steeple on a hill
* finding a path with no footprints
* finding a path with many footprints
* cellars lined with jars of preserves

I love going to Aunt Ann's for Christmas. She decorates everything from the bushes outside to the paper towel holder in the kitchen. She cooks the most wonderful dishes, and her home should be featured in *House Beautiful*. Not only is her home wonderful; she is wonderful—the most giving, charitable person to ever exist.

CONNIE JOHNSON

* "You stand a better chance of getting a kiss from both friends or strangers than any other time."
* "Young men will see visions, old men will dream dreams."
* red blankets in sleigh ride carriages
* a Christmas moon shining on snow
* the reflection of stained glass in gold globe ornaments
* little girls telling their new dolls it's time for bed
* babies dragging their blankies
* cold cider in a goblet
* Grandpa sweeping the snow off his porch for Christmas company
* a "Charlie Brown" Christmas tree
* "gold and myrrh and frankincense"
* a bale of hay and Christmas carrots for the deer
* a basket of herb teas
* a Bass and Rankin Christmas cartoon
* red as a symbol for sacrifice; we remember that Jesus saved the world
* gloves with jingle bells on the fingers
* the Salvation Army singers and band
* a real sheep dog in the Christmas play
* a Christmas tins collection under the Christmas tree
* snow pets
* a big cozy rocking chair

ANGELS WE HAVE HEARD ON HIGH

Angels we have heard on high
Sweetly singing o'er the plains,
And the mountains in reply
Echoing their joyous strains.
Gloria, in excelsis Deo!
Gloria, in excelsis Deo!
Shepherds, why this jubilee?
Why your joyous strains prolong?
What the gladsome tidings be
Which inspire your heavenly song?
Gloria, in excelsis Deo!
Gloria, in excelsis Deo!
Come to Bethlehem and see
Christ whose birth the angels sing;
Come, adore on bended knee,
Christ the Lord, the newborn King.
Gloria, in excelsis Deo!
Gloria, in excelsis Deo!
See Him in a manger laid,
Whom the choirs of angels praise;
Mary, Joseph, lend your aid,
While our hearts in love we raise.

TRANSLATED BY JAMES CHADWICK

* having all your shopping done ahead of time
* waiting until the last minute to shop
* "Guess who?"
* colored Christmas lights on a fountain
* a big mushy snowball: one that missed me, one that hit my brother—and went down his neck—and made him yell
* a bowl of nuts in the shell
* a bright shooting star
* a caroling hayride through the neighborhood
* a Christmas tree by a spiral staircase
* a catnip mouse for kitty

Christmas is making something for someone I love. Every handmade gift includes hours spent thinking about that person, what they would like, how I am going to make it special, and how much they will enjoy the labor of love.

SUSAN CONDER

Scents of Christmas

* mountain air
* an ocean breeze
* bayberry candles
* the smell of apple pies baking
* cedar chests
* lavender soap
* wet boots
* chamomile
* wet pets
* ski wax
* Dove dishwashing liquid
* the smell of orchids in Florida
* an outdoor barbecue in the Southwest
* a barn full of fresh hay
* the smell of salt sea air

* a Christmas carol sing-along
* a certain sleepy sigh
* snow on top of the ski lift
* baby sleeping holding a stuffed animal
* a Christmas tree display by the top of the mall escalator
* an angel watching over our sleeping child
* cookie stars
* a chickadee on a bare branch
* a children's Bible
* a Christmas baby
* red and white Christmas roses
* the quiet hills of Bethlehem
* a Christmas-light-display star
* Grandpa snoring in front of the TV
* a chuck wagon dinner at a Texas dude ranch
* a covered parking space
* little girls in green velvet dresses
* "he had a round face an a little round belly that shook when he laughed like a bowl full of jelly"
* cookies for Santa on a big plate
* a Christmas tree for birds
* a craft sale before Christmas
* gingerbread men with raisin eyes
* a dated Christmas ornament
* a dining table loaded with favorite foods

The star they had seen in the east went ahead of them until it stopped over the place where the child was. When they saw the star, they were overjoyed. ... On coming to the house, they saw the child with his mother Mary, and they bowed down and worshiped him. Then they opened their treasures and presented him with gifts of gold and of incense and of myrrh.

MATTHEW 2:9–11

To see his star is good, but to see his face is better.

DWIGHT L. MOODY

* a dollhouse that is decorated for Christmas
* a dozen Christmas roses from my sweetheart
* red and green sugar sprinkles
* a driveway outlined by Christmas lights
* a Christmas tree in the corner of the living room
* a family gift exchange
* snow globes with:
  * Victorian figurines
  * Nativity scenes
  * children
  * Santa
  * animals
  * cartoon characters
  * houses
  * farms
  * Christmas trees
  * silver snowflakes
  * white snowflakes
  * multicolored snowflakes
  * ice-skaters
  * ballerinas
* cookies for the band parents' fund-raiser
* "holy infant so tender and mild"
* a feather kitten teaser
* a forty-five-year-old "kid" opening presents

* a full planner page in December
* Grandpa playing the organ
* a Christmas tree on a porch
* red and green M&M's
* corn bread with honey
* a Glamour Shots session
* the neighborhood lighting contest
* reading the Christmas story from the family Bible together
* a glass nativity scene
* a glowing fireplace: red coals, the snapping and crackling of fire, being really warm on the side toward the fire
* alpine ski lodges
* fleece pullovers
* Hershey's Kisses with almonds in gold wrappers
* lead crystal Christmas tree candy jars
* the way colored Christmas lights look when you scrunch up your eyes to make them blurry
* playing soft Christmas music to go to sleep by
* Christmas plum pudding
* The Oxford Boys Choir Christmas Eve service
* "The Little Match Girl"
* Christmas memory books
* *A Child's Christmas in Wales*
* a present from Victoria's Secret

* "I bring you good tidings of great joy ..."
* Cracker Barrel rocking chairs
* a gold chain for Grandma's reading glasses
* a grand ballroom with a huge Christmas tree
* snow forts for a family snowball war
* a handwritten invitation
* a gold ink pen
* Grandpa playing Santa Claus for the grandchildren
* a heated garage
* a hello meow from kitty
* a Christmas tree set up in the middle of the ice arena, with skaters turning around it
* a Hershey's Kiss wreath
* a holiday wedding with Christmas colors
* a home fellowship group joining hands
* the Nativity story from Luke 2
* a horse-drawn sleigh ride
* a hot tub: inside with candles burning all around, outside with snow falling, drinking warm cider, drinking cold punch, having it to yourself, sharing with your spouse
* "I Heard the Bells on Christmas Day"
* a kitten curled up on Grandma's lap
* Grandpa and Grandma telling the old family stories after dinner
* Cracker Jack
* a lead crystal vase

Merry Christmas to All Creatures Great and Small

* white ducks in the barnyard
* *All Dogs Go to Heaven*
* saltwater fish tanks:
  * zebra fish
  * pencil fish
  * sea horses
  * clown fish
  * blue sharks
  * sea anemones
  * coral
  * catfish
  * striped angels
* swans on the pond
* freshwater fish tanks:
  * guppies
  * mollies
  * hatchet fish
  * goldfish
  * fantails
  * big brown snails
* mallard ducks on the creek
* *101 Dalmatians*

* a letter to Santa
* a lick from kitty's scratchy tongue
* a list of the gifts God's blessed us with during the past year
* sleeping really late
* a little black lamb
* a living manger scene at our church
* a long walk on a starry evening
* cranberry muffins
* Grandmother's scarves and shawls that "keep the drafts away"
* "I love setting up my Nativity scene each year and thinking about what it would have been like to be present at the birth of Jesus."
* a golden angel halo
* a Looney Tunes Christmas tree
* snow angels on the front lawn
* a manger scene carved in wax
* the love of God shown through the birth of the Savior
* a Mary and Child soft sculpture in a quilt
* the movie *White Christmas*
* little girls in red velvet dresses
* a miniature tree centerpiece
* a model stable made from Popsicle sticks
* a mother's lullaby
* a Nativity carved from wood
* a new collar for the dog

GO, TELL IT ON THE MOUNTAIN

Go, tell it on the mountain,
Over the hills and everywhere
Go, tell it on the mountain,
That Jesus Christ is born.
While shepherds kept their watching
Over silent flocks by night
Behold throughout the heavens
There shone a holy light.
Go, tell it on the mountain,
Over the hills and everywhere
Go, tell it on the mountain,
That Jesus Christ is born.

JOHN WESLEY WORK JR.

* a new hairdo for the holiday
* a new kitten for Christmas:
  * short hair
  * long hair, tiger
  * all white
  * all black with a white chin
  * black-and-white spotted
  * Persian
  * Siamese
  * Maine coon cat
  * orange tabby
  * Russian Blue
  * Angora
  * Balinese
  * mystery mix kitten
* singing Christmas carols at a nursing home
* a new study Bible
* grandmother teaching us folk carols from her native land
* a real bird's nest found in the Christmas tree
* a new watch: Mickey Mouse watch, Caravel, Rolex, Timex
* a newborn falling asleep in a baby swing
* ski tracks
* a palomino pony pulling kids on a sled
* a parakeet that whistles "Jingle Bells"
* a patient old draft horse munching his Christmas carrots
* a plateful of cookies after caroling

* a puppy dreaming under the tree
* a real baby to play Jesus in the manger
* a recording of cats meowing, "We Wish You a Merry Christmas"
* grandmas with embroidered handkerchiefs
* "I'm Dreaming of a White Christmas"
* peppermint tea

MISTLETOE

Sitting under the mistletoe
(Pale green, fairy mistletoe)
One last candle burning low,
All the sleepy dancers gone,
Just one candle burning on,
Shadows lurking everywhere:
Someone came, and kissed me there.
Tired as I was; my head would go
Nodding under the mistletoe
(Pale green, fairy mistletoe)
No footstep came, no voice, but only,
Just as I sat there, sleepy, lonely,
Stooped in the still and shadowy air,
Lips unseen—and kissed me there.

WALTER DE LAMARE

* silvery silent stars
* making Christmas ornaments in Sunday school
* little girls in ballet costumes
* a red and green welcome mat
* cranberry salad
* love notes in my stocking
* a relish tray: dill deli pickles, baby sweet pickles, pimento-stuffed green olives, black olives, celery, broccoli, pickled cauliflower, pickled baby corn ears
* a romantic walk while holding hands in the starlight
* a rustic stable
* a shepherd campfire
* "Buffalo Girl, won't you come out tonight."
* cream puffs
* a silk rose Christmas tree

One of my most vivid Christmas memories is of the smell of oranges. We always got an orange and nuts and sometimes an apple and hard candy in our stockings. We didn't have fancy Christmas stockings, so my four brothers, two sisters and I would raid Dad's dresser drawer for socks to tape on the woodwork of the living room door. After Christmas my dad always had seven really long, stretched-out socks to wear!

KAREN SMITH

THE TWELVE DAYS OF CHRISTMAS

On the first day of Christmas,
My true love gave to me:
A partridge in a pear tree.

On the second day of Christmas,
My true love gave to me:
Two turtle doves, and a partridge in a pear tree.

On the third day of Christmas,
My true love gave to me:
Three French hens, two turtle doves and a partridge
in a pear tree.

On the forth day of Christmas,
My true love gave to me:
Four calling birds, three French hens, two turtle doves and a
partridge in a pear tree.

On the fifth day of Christmas,
My true love gave to me:
Five golden rings, four calling birds, three French hens, two
turtle doves and a partridge in a pear tree.

On the sixth day of Christmas,
My true love gave to me:
Six geese a-laying, five golden rings, four calling birds, three
French hens, two turtle doves and a partridge in a pear tree.

On the seventh day of Christmas,
My true love gave to me:
Seven swans a-swimming, six geese a-laying,
five golden rings, four calling birds, three French hens, two
turtle doves and a partridge in a pear tree.

On the eight day of Christmas,
My true love gave to me:
Eight maids a-milking, seven swans a-swimming, six geese
a-laying, five golden rings, four calling birds, three French
hens, two turtle doves and a partridge in a pear tree.

On the ninth day of Christmas,
My true love gave to me:
Nine ladies dancing, eight maids a-milking, seven swans a-
swimming, six geese a-laying, five golden rings, four calling
birds, three French hens, two turtle doves and a partridge in
a pear tree.

On the tenth day of Christmas,
My true love gave to me:
Ten lords a-leaping, nine ladies dancing, eight maids a-
milking, seven swans a-swimming, six geese a-laying, five
golden rings, four calling birds, three French hens, two turtle
doves and a partridge in a pear tree.

On the eleventh day of Christmas,
My true love gave to me:
Eleven pipers piping, ten lords a-leaping, nine ladies danc-
ing, eight maids a-milking, seven swans a-swimming, six
geese a-laying, five golden rings, four calling birds, three
French hens, two turtle doves and a partridge in a pear tree.

On the twelfth day of Christmas,
My true love gave to me:
Twelve drummers drumming, eleven pipers piping, ten lords
a-leaping, nine ladies dancing, eight maids a-milking, seven
swans a-swimming, six geese a-laying, five golden rings,
four calling birds, three French hens, two turtle doves and a
partridge in a pear tree.

ENGLISH TRADITIONAL CAROL

My favorite Christmas memory . . .

_____

_____

_____

_____

_____

_____

_____

_____

_____

_____

_____

_____

_____

_____

_____

_____

_____

_____

_____

_____

_____

Romance

* doing nothing all day together
* holding hands with my sweetheart in a crowded mall and feeling as if we are all alone
* a playful snowball fight
* she always knows what color I look best in
* writing Christmas letters as a couple for the first time
* writing Christmas letters as a couple for the twentieth time
* a silver bracelet with our names on it
* "I love beating my husband at Scrabble, and he loves beating me at chess."
* touching shoulders with my sweetheart as we wash dishes
* a teddy bear couple that looks like the two of us
* a toast to us
* milk and rose bubble bath
* a wreath of red satin hearts
* knowing we will remember this moment years from now
* a dated ornament for our first Christmas together
* a dated ornament for our twenty-fifth Christmas together

* a ski chalet
* a sky so black and the stars so silver against it
* a snow-covered yard lit by multicolored lights
* "It Came upon the Midnight Clear"
* a snowflake alighting on a child's eyelash
* Grandma's white Christmas tree with pink ornaments
* making gingerbread houses and eating the house parts as you go along
* silver-star hairpins
* little cousins dressed up for a Nativity scene singing, "Away in a Manger"
* cross-country skiing on a bright, still night

Be merry all,
Be merry all,
With holly dress the festive hall;
Prepare the song,
the feast, the ball,
To welcome merry Christmas.

W.R. Spencer

* baby sleeping in an antique wooden cradle
* a spirit of thanksgiving
* a sports theme Christmas tree
* a star on top of the tree:
  * gold
  * silver
  * glass
  * tinsel
  * illuminated frame
  * papier-mâché
  * origami
* a stocking stuffed with candy:
  * all-day suckers
  * Tootsie Rolls
  * candy canes
  * gummy toys
  * Jolly Ranchers
  * licorice
  * Dum-Dums
  * Raisnettes
  * Nestle's Crunch bars
  * Good 'N Plenty
  * Almond Joy
  * Twizzlers
  * rainbow gum
  * jawbreakers
* a stone-hewn fireplace
* a surprise getaway weekend together
* a thankful prayer to God for family
* a tiered stack of poinsettias in the shape of a Christmas tree

When the angels had left them and gone into heaven, the shepherds said to one another, "Let's go to Bethlehem and see this thing that has happened, which the Lord has told us about."

So they hurried off and found Mary and Joseph, and the baby, who was lying in the manger.

When they had seen him, they spread the word concerning what had been told them about this child, and all who heard it were amazed at what the shepherds said to them.

LUKE 2:15–18

The feet of the humblest may walk in the
    fields
Where the feet of the holiest have trod.
This, this is the marvel to mortals
    revealed,
When the silvery trumpets of
      Christmas have pealed,
That mankind are the children of God.

PHILLIPS BROOKS

* a time to rejoice
* a tin full of cheese-, caramel-, and butter-flavored popcorn
* a tinsel halo for baby
* cutting down the Christmas tree
* a real donkey at the Nativity scene
* Grandma's silk-flowered church hat
* a toast to family and friends
* a toddler carefully touching the fur of a new kitten
* cross-stitch ornaments
* silver seraphim songs
* a toy for Spot under the tree
* a tree ornament with the Nativity scene in it
* baby's favorite blanket
* Dad checking the skating pond's ice to see if it's thick enough
* a trip to the Christmas tree farm
* a vase of Christmas roses on the table
* decorating the Christmas tree in a new theme we've never tried before
* decorating the Christmas tree in the same way we all love and remember
* "joyful and triumphant"
* pine bough wreaths
* a Victorian angel on top of the tree
* a walk around the frozen lake
* baked custard

HARK! THE HERALD ANGELS SING

Hark! The herald angels sing,
"Glory to the newborn King;
Peace on earth, and mercy mild,
God and sinners reconciled!"
Joyful, all ye nations rise,
Join the triumph of the skies;
With th'angelic host proclaim,
"Christ is born in Bethlehem!"
Hark! the herald angels sing,
"Glory to the newborn King!"
Christ, by highest heav'n adored;
Christ the everlasting Lord;
Late in time, behold Him come,
Offspring of a virgin's womb.

Veiled in flesh the Godhead see;
Hail th'incarnate Deity,
Pleased with us in flesh to dwell,
Jesus our Emmanuel.
Hark! the herald angels sing,
"Glory to the newborn King!"
Hail the heavenly Prince of Peace!
Hail the Sun of Righteousness!
Light and life to all He brings,
Ris'n with healing in His wings.
Mild He lays His glory by,
Born that man no more may die.
Born to raise the sons of earth,
Born to give them second birth.
Hark! the herald angels sing,
"Glory to the newborn King!"

CHARLES WESLEY

Christmas in England

Several Christmas customs began in England. One is the use of Christmas trees. This was made popular during the reign of Queen Victoria and Prince Albert. Prince Albert came from the country of Germany and missed his native practice of bringing in trees to place on the tables in the house, therefore one Christmas the royal couple brought a tree inside the Palace and decorated it with apples and other pretty items.

Another custom is what is known as Boxing Day. It is celebrated the first weekday after Christmas. What this means is that small wrapped boxes with food and sweets, or small gifts, or coins are given to anyone who comes calling that day.

Our custom of caroling comes from Britain's custom where groups of serenaders called "waits" travel from house to house singing carols, which means "songs of joy." These nineteeth century songs are still among today's most beloved Christmas music.

* alternative Christmas trees: a blown-glass tree, a big grapevine cone or even a person!
* Dad snoring under the newspaper
* little boys making loud engine sounds for their new cars
* "It wouldn't be the same without you!"
* Dad pointing out the constellations
* a walk on Clearwater beach
* a warm bubble bath
* baby's first Bible
* making paper chains with little ones
* a white artificial tree with silver ornaments
* little boys in cowboy boots
* Grandma's pantry
* a white horse with red and green ribbons
* a wooden Nativity stable with straw on the roof
* "Just what I always wanted!"
* a youth group guitar service
* acolytes in red robes
* silver napkin rings
* Advent candles
* maple sugar candy
* after-Christmas-dinner nap
* all the stage moms at the Christmas play
* thinking up new ways to wrap gifts
* thinking up new places to hide gifts
* dining room table leaf insert
* almond banket
* pine sap from freshly cut evergreens

Good has given me a tangible reminder of the surpassing wonder of the gift of his coming to earth, in my daughter Mary Noelle (Molly) who was given to us on Christmas Morning 1987.

DONALD L. WILLIAMSON

Christmas is the one time a year when prisoners are most like ordinary people. In many prisons there is no limit on the amount of food an inmate can receive, so many inmates receive grocery bags stuffed with all kinds of foods. Things like peanuts, cookies, cakes, sausage, ham, turkey, cheeses, and a host of other goodies seen only once a year. Of course, no one person can consume all of what he receives, so, almost in spite of themselves, the inmates who do receive food end up sharing it with those who do not have friends or family to bring them anything. It is an incredible sight to see.

GREG WILLIAMSON

The Meaning of the Twelve Days of Christmas:

✳ God himself is the generous "true love" who gives good gifts to his people

✳ two turtledoves stand for the Old and New Testaments.

✳ three French hens are for faith, hope, and love that never fails

✳ four calling birds are the four Gospels in the New Testament, Matthew, Mark, Luke, and John

✳ five golden rings are the first five books of the Old Testament.

✳ six geese a-laying stand for the six days of God's creation of the world

✳ seven swans a-swimming are the seven gifts of the Holy Spirit

✳ eight maids a-milking stand for the eight beatitudes of Christ's teaching in Matthew

✳ nine ladies dancing are for nine types of angels

✳ ten lords a-leaping stand for the Ten Commandments

✳ eleven pipers piping are for the eleven faithful apostles

✳ twelve drummers drumming stand for the twelve elements of faith in the Apostles' Creed

* milk shakes:
  * malted
  * chocolate
  * vanilla
  * jamocha
  * eggnog
  * peppermint
  * orange
  * fortified breakfast shakes
  * peanut butter and chocolate
  * banana
  * peach
  * with whipped cream and a cherry
  * fruit smoothies
* getting so many toys you don't know which to play with first
* babies in high chairs
* Grandma singing her favorite carol
* an all-doll Christmas tree
* an angel concert for shepherds
* seven-layer salad
* family photos in front of the Christmas tree
* babies who like to play with the boxes that their toys came in more than the toy itself
* Fisher Price record players

* baked ham with pineapple slices
* dinner at the mall food court:
  * large-size pizza
  * bagels
  * wonton soup and egg rolls
  * fried chicken
  * hamburgers and French fries
* silver illuminated Christmas trees on top of tall buildings
* lights as a symbol for joy, purity, and perfection
* pinecone wreaths
* an animated tree singing corny songs
* all the opportunities for giving a hug
* all the opportunities for getting a hug
* dog dishes with "Good Dog" lettering
* an antique doll display:
  * Raggedy Ann and Andy
  * Shirley Temple dolls
  * 1960's Barbie and Ken
  * Chatty Cathy and Susie Smart
  * Tiny Tears doll
* an eggnog toast pronounced by Grandpa
* an engraved invitation
* eternal joy and peace
* an illuminated cross on a hillside

IT CAME UPON THE MIDNIGHT CLEAR

It came upon the midnight clear,
That glorious song of old,
From angels bending near the earth
To touch their harps of gold:
Peace on the earth, good will to men,
From heaven's all-gracious King!
The world in solemn stillness lay
To hear the angels sing.

Still through the cloven skies they come
with peaceful wings unfurled;
and still their heavenly music floats
O'er all the weary world;
Above its sad and lowly plains
They bend on hovering wing,
And ever o'er its Babel sounds
The blessed angels sing.

EDMUND H. SEARS

* bagels:
  * blueberry
  * tomato herb
  * parmesan cheese
  * pizza
  * rye
  * sea salt
  * with cream cheese
  * whole wheat
  * plain
  * egg
  * sesame seed
  * caraway seed
  * cinnamon raisin
  * ultimate mix
* lighting candles together on Christmas Eve
* baguettes
* baking powder biscuits
* baklava
* Balderdash
* ballet shoe ornaments
* baking a birthday cake for Jesus
* banana nut bread
* dogs going up the ski gondola with their owners in the Alps

* Barbie Christmas tree ornaments
* barn kittens sitting on a horse's back to keep warm
* basil
* silver candy dishes
* baskets of Michigan apples
* bayberry
* Grandma in her kerchief
* beadwork bracelets
* beanbag chairs in the family room
* being a Secret Santa to someone at work or church
* Belgian waffles
* big aluminum coffee percolators
* fur coats
* long scarves wrapped around little ones
* lemon trees with white lights
* old-fashioned bulb lights
* everyone at the family Christmas gathering smells so good because they are all wearing the perfumes and colognes they got for presents
* taking your new doll to Christmas at Grandma's to show to your cousins
* grown-ups enjoying playing with the toys that they bought for their kids

Snow piled high. Frost biting at the corners of windows. Warm homes brimming with love. All of these things contribute to the joy of Christmas. But none compare to the gift our heavenly Father gave that night so long ago. The lights on the tree are his birthday candles. The endless stack of gifts beneath it are like the showers of gifts He pours out on us every day. Like the mother who couldn't remain within her budget for the love she wanted to show her children that morning—that is what Christ has in store for his children. Only he doesn't have a budget!

STEVE ROSINSKI

I love getting together with my whole family on Christmas Eve to celebrate together. The younger cousins dress up, and we have a Nativity scene and sing "Away in a Manger." Then we have a birthday cake for Jesus, and we sing "Happy Birthday" to him. After opening presents and eating dinner, we go to the 11:00 candlelight service at our church. The service is always amazing, and at the end the choir circles around the church, and we all sing "Silent Night" with a descant of children singing "peace" along with the hymn. It's awesome!

BRIANNA ESSWEIN

I'll Be Home for Christmas

❋ laughter on my sister's face
❋ the creaking of the wooden floors in my parents' home
❋ playing board games and cards
❋ signing our family Christmas cards together
❋ reading Dickens' Christmas stories aloud
❋ time together
❋ old family movies and videos:
   ❋ my mother's first steps
   ❋ Christmases past
   ❋ clips of great-grandparents
   ❋ family vacations
   ❋ new baby videos of everyone
   ❋ wedding videos
❋ ice-skating on our favorite pond together
❋ a big pile of boots in the foyer
❋ the old house full of people sleeping in every room and on all the couches and floors
❋ snowmen that look like family members
❋ hearing the doorbell ring on Christmas Eve and everyone yelling, "I'll get it!"
❋ teenagers racing for the phone
❋ the sound of a familiar car's engine coming in the driveway

COME, THOU LONG EXPECTED JESUS

Come, Thou long expected Jesus
Born to set Thy people free;
From our fears and sins release us,
Let us find our rest in Thee.
Israel's strength and consolation,
Hope of all the earth Thou art;
Dear desire of every nation,
Joy of every longing heart.
Born Thy people to deliver,
Born a child and yet a King,
Born to reign in us forever,
Now Thy gracious kingdom bring.
By Thine own eternal Spirit
Rule in all our hearts alone;
By Thine all sufficient merit,
Raise us to Thy glorious throne.

CHARLES WESLEY

* "let loving hearts enthrone Him"
* big pots of soft cheddar cheese
* Santa mugs full of steaming drinks
* big Texas grapefruit wrapped in green tissue paper
* silly lyrics we make up when we forget the words to carols
* generous tumblers full of punch
* bingo
* kitty's carpet house
* dogs with red kerchiefs over their collars
* "Mickey's Christmas Carol"

HYMN ON THE MORNING OF CHRIST'S NATIVITY

Ring out, ye crystal spheres
Once bless our human ears
(If ye have power to touch our sense so)
And let your silver chime
Move in melodious time,
And let the base of Heaven's deep organ blow;
And with your ninefold harmony
Make up full consort of the angelic symphony.

JOHN MILTON

* bird ornaments with real feathers:
    * cardinals
    * bluebirds
    * doves
    * peacocks
* "Mary" and "Joseph" having irreconcilable differences before the play
* Bird-in-Hand, Pennsylvania's Amish gift shops
* soap-on-a-rope
* Dad pretending he's never seen soap-on-a-rope before
* Grandma calling for us to wake up
* blown-glass ornaments:
    * swans
    * skaters
    * horses
    * unicorns
    * bears
    * snowflakes
    * sailboats
    * poodles
    * reindeer
    * Santa and elves
* blue and gold balls on a tree
* boats with Christmas lights gliding in the bay
* Bob Cratchet
* boot prints going in all directions
* shops with homespun gifts in Gatlinburg
* Borden's eggnog

To us a child is born,
* to us a son is given,*
*   and the government will be on his shoulders.*
And he will be called
*   Wonderful Counselor, Mighty God,*
*   Everlasting Father, Prince of Peace.*

ISAIAH 9:6

I vividly see Jesus, King of the Universe, leaving his throne in heaven, perhaps hugging his Father good-bye, and coming to dwell here on earth. What a gift to us! Packaged in the body of a beautiful infant boy was the Savior of the World.

For God so loved the world that he gave his one and only Son, that whoever believes in him shall not perish but have eternal life.

JOHN 3:16

* Bowl games on TV
* "merry, merry, merry, merry Christmas"
* Boy Scouts ice-skating on the pond
* Boyd's bears
* brass fireplace tools
* bread machines
* breakfast served in bed
* breath clouds on a cold day
* bright Christmas trumpets
* bringing in fresh firewood
* "Mother, May I?"
* brioche
* Christmas ornaments that look handmade
* Christmas ornaments that look store-bought
* brittle candy without the peanuts
* dogs with Santa hats or antlers attached to them
* brown sugar
* shopping for that special gift you know they'll just love and watching that special someone's face light up when they open your gift
* kitty purring on the couch
* Bugs Bunny, Daffy Duck, Elmer Fudd, Wylie Coyote, Taz, Road Runner ornaments
* bumper riding
* bunny blankets with zippers

❋ Burl Ives singing "Silver and Gold"

❋ "My house is your house."

❋ burning the Christmas wrap in the fireplace

❋ businesses decorated for the season

❋ visiting Omar the camel at the local petting zoo

❋ Christmas carols played on a harp

❋ "What is it you want, Mary? You want the moon? Just say the word and I'll throw a lasso around it and pull it down for you."

❋ getting a much needed vacation from work

❋ no tube socks for Christmas

❋ serving Christmas tea with a silver tea set

❋ watching "The Sound of Music" on Christmas afternoon

❋ going to sleep with your new stuffed animal on Christmas night

❋ those plastic pointy elf ears I had to wear in my 4th grade Christmas play

❋ being amazed at how much kids grow when you haven't seen them since the previous Christmas

❋ red ribbons tied in black hair

❋ hearing the song "Feliz Navidad" about a million times on the radio

In high school, I was on the yearbook staff. One evening in December, my friend Dawn and I were waiting for a school board meeting to end so we could photograph the board for the yearbook. There were several other people from the community also waiting to be admitted into the meeting once the closed-door session was finished. The room was so silent that it was rather uncomfortable. So, my friend Dawn, being the nutty girl that she is, piped up. "Hey, does anybody want to see my shirt light up?" The others in the room looked at each other and us with sheepish grins and nodded. Dawn happily flipped a little switch that was sewed into her shirt and turned herself into a walking Christmas light display. Her sweatshirt had Christmas lights sewn into it and they began to blink and flash and generally fill the room with giggles. Thank goodness for Dawn and her light-up sweatshirt—the perfect icebreaker!

MOLLY DETWEILER

* "a partridge in a pear tree"
* buttermilk pancakes: blueberry and banana
* passing the serving plates around
* buying new Christmas ornaments
* quilted Christmas stockings
* drinking the Coca-Cola left for Santa
* Grandma and Grandpa's family photo album
* paper lanterns
* cactus Christmas trees
* "nine ladies dancing"
* putting makeup on little lambs for the Christmas play
* calling family far away and passing the phone around
* calm moments
* shopping bags with handles
* camels with royal saddles and gold fringe
* driving through the Smoky Mountains
* cameras:
  * instant print
  * Cannon Sure Shot
  * Olympus slimline style
  * Minolta zoom lens
  * Pentax 35mm
  * old-fashioned "brownie" box
  * Kodak APS
* kitty pouncing on your bare toes

WHAT CHILD IS THIS?

What child is this, who, laid to rest
On Mary's lap, is sleeping?
Whom angels greet with anthems sweet,
While shepherds watch are keeping?
This, this is Christ the King,
Whom shepherds guard and angels sing:
Haste, haste to bring him laud,
The Babe, the Son of Mary!

So bring Him incense, gold, and myrrh,
Come peasant king to own Him,
The King of kings, salvation brings,
Let loving hearts enthrone Him.
Raise, raise the song on high,
The Virgin sings her lullaby:
Joy, joy, for Christ is born,
The Babe, the Son of Mary!

ENGLISH TRADITIONAL CAROL

Snowmen and Other Creatures

* hobbits:
  * Frodo
  * Samwise
  * Pippen
* Ma and Pa snowmen
* snowmen in wool hats
* Narnia creatures:
  * Aslan
  * Mr. and Mrs. Beaver
  * Mr. Tumnus
  * the giants
  * unicorns
  * the dwarves
  * Puddleglum
  * Sea-People
* Mother Goose and storybook characters:
  * Humpty Dumpty
  * Red Riding Hood
  * Mary and her lamb
  * Tom Thumb
  * Hanzel and Gretel
  * Thumbelina
* skier snowmen
* toddlers' little tiny snowmen
* half-melted snowmen

This is Christmas: not the tinsel, not the giving and receiving, not even the carols, but the humble heart that receives anew that wondrous gift, the Christ.

FRANK McKIBBEN

The hinge of history is on the door of a Bethlehem stable.

RALPH W. SOCKMAN

Thus we can always know that men could live with goodwill and understanding for each other, because one day in each year the little Divine Prince of Peace still compels them to do it.

CHARLES JEREMIAH WELLS

* candid photos:
  * opening presents
  * putting together toys
  * eating together
  * arriving at the front door
  * caroling (and everyone's mouths are open in the picture!)
* candles in the window
* eating the apples my children left for the reindeer
* puppy's comfy basket
* palm trees full of seagulls and Christmas lights
* ornaments with names of towns or landmarks
* kitty chasing a yarn ball
* candy canes disappearing from the tree
* "Do You Hear What I Hear?"
* candy canes for after-dinner mints
* canned fruit:
  * mandarin oranges
  * fruit cocktail with cherries
  * apricots
  * peaches
  * pears

* opening the last window on the Advent calendar
* "Noel, Noel, Noel, Noel, born is the King of Israel"
* caramel corn
* shepherds in bathrobes
* caraway
* card games:
  * hearts,
  * 7-Up,
  * Go Fish
  * pinochle
  * bridge
  * canasta
  * Mille Bournes
  * Uno
  * Old Maid
* carolers in winter costumes at Disney World
* carousel horse and animal ornaments:
  * racers
  * prancers
  * knights' horses
  * giraffes
  * pigs
* little kids rolling big snowballs
* trails all over the yard from little kids rolling big snowballs

Christmas in Russia

Russia has someone named Babouschka, who would bring gifts for the children. The tradition says that she failed to give food and shelter to the three wise men and so she now searches the countryside searching for the baby Jesus, visiting all children giving gifts as she goes. Santa was known as Saint Nicholas but during communist rule it was changed to Grandfather Frost, wearing a blue outfit instead of red. Today in Russia, St. Nicolas is making a come back.

* "come, let us adore Him, Christ the Lord"
* opening the front door and smelling Christmas breads baking
* cars with Christmas lights on them
* carved wooden serving bowls
* Castle Risk
* eating the icing first out of Oreos
* cat dishes with "Spoiled Cat" lettering
* "O Come All Ye Faithful"
* catching the "mouse" that nibbled the corners off the chocolates, looking for a caramel
* cathedral cookies (stained-glass window cookies)
* "eight maids a-milking"
* Cave of the Winds with Christmas lights
* eggs Benedict
* CD cases and racks
* shepherds following angels
* ceiling fans
* kittens playing with the tinsel
* Celtic Christmas music
* Elvis Christmas ornaments
* checkers
* opening presents while watching the Christmas parades with the kids
* cheerful crowds of people shopping
* "Every time a bell rings, an angel gets its wings."
* children catching snowflakes on their tongues

* cheese corn
* chenille pillows
* Cherry 7-Up
* cherub toes
* chess
* chewy toys for puppy:
    * rubber bones
    * rawhide shoes
    * stretchy pull straps
    * terry cloth stuffed animals
* Chia Pets
* everyone pitching in to prepare and clean up after decorating
* shepherd dogs
* gold garlands
* opening presents while watching the bowl games
* "O Come, O Come Emmanuel"

Christmas is sharing the gift of the Christ child in a tangible way—giving time, talents, and mostly the joy of Jesus that is within. At Christmas giving is unquestioned—it is welcome and expected. It is the opportunity to live our heart's desires every day. I give the gifts, sing the songs, share the stories, live the love, and praise the Prince. It is my favorite time of the year!

When my brother and I were small, we would begin an elaborate plan on how we were going to sneak out and see our presents on Christmas morning. Each day for a month we would have a secret meeting to go over our plans. We were like little Christmas secret agents. In the end, though, we would end up simply tip-toeing into our parents' room and asking if it was okay to open presents yet. For all our espionage planning, we were too chicken to actually sneak out and look at our presents without permission!

MOLLY DETWEILER

As a child, Christmas was magical—the ornately decorated tree surrounded by an abundance of gifts, a dining table covered with my favorite foods, with the light of a few flickering candles. Outside the house was the otherworldly, snow-covered yard, and through the lightly falling snow I could see the multicolored lights of a neighbor's house. As an adult, Christmas remains magical, but for different reasons. People seem to change. There are more smiles, more happy human sounds, and a general feeling of joy. As a Christian, Christmas reminds me that One was born and lived and died and now lives again so that I might live forever with him in eternal joy and peace.

BILL COLBURN

Favorite Presents Given and Received

* *Goodnight Moon*
* fuzzy dice for the kids' car
* *Treasure Island*
* telephone credit cards
* Shadow boxes and curio shelves
* Spiderman comic books
* photo screens
* *The Little Prince*
* clock radio CD player
* glass party dishes
* *Madeline*
* a red tool box
* a box of hair barrettes
* portable computer
* the big box of Crayola crayons with a sharpener in the back
* *The Velveteen Rabbit*
* Nancy Drew mysteries
* Hardy Boys adventure books
* a garage door opener
* digital camera
* antique quilt rack
* a book of chore coupons
* a new place setting of our good china
* salt and pepper grinders

* leather jacket
* nylon jogging suits
* a big toy box
* a play tent
* an art set:
  * watercolors
  * Play Dough
  * Magic Markers
  * crayons
  * scissors
  * paste
* travel tickets:
  * a cruise
  * a plane trip
  * railroad tour
  * resort vacation
* kittens in a box
* golf equipment:
  * putters
  * irons
  * drivers
  * Big Bertha
  * Titlest balls
  * club covers
  * Spaulding bags
  * bag of tees
  * glow-in-the-dark balls
  * golf hats, ties, shirts, socks, shorts, shoes

* old-fashioned wooden case radios
* miniature jukeboxes
* neon artwork
* ballet slippers and costume
* tap shoes
* basketballs, footballs, golf balls, playground balls
* Ping-Pong table and paddles
* paper dolls:
  * Betsey McCall
  * American Girl
  * Barbie
* Sesame Street or Muppet stuffed dolls:
  * Kermit
  * Miss Piggy
  * Grover
  * Elmo
  * Cookie Monster
  * Oscar the Grouch
  * Bert and Ernie
  * Gonzo
* a toy tool bench
* plastic spring horse that neighs
* Camelot dolls and figurines:
  * King Arthur
  * Sir Lancelot
  * Guinevere
  * Merlin

❋ an old-fashioned hearth screen
❋ an olive branch, the symbol of peace on Earth
❋ an outdoor light display at a farm
❋ Grandma Leah's homemade black walnut caramels
❋ silver garlands
❋ dog sweaters and booties: plaid, tuxedo, woolly, fleece or matching their owner's
❋ angel candles
❋ animal crackers
❋ announcing a Christmas engagement
❋ antique high chairs
❋ any warm Christmas cookies fresh from the oven
❋ anyone else volunteering for dish duty
❋ appetizer tray:
    ❋ stuffed dates
    ❋ nachos and salsa dip
    ❋ crackers with cheese
    ❋ mini sandwiches
    ❋ rolled tortilla sandwiches
❋ bread bowls with spinach dip
❋ apple fritters
❋ arranging the manger scene for church with family and friends
❋ Aspen Mountain artisan village
❋ automatic starter keys so you don't need to go out to start the car
❋ silver dragoon balls on cookies

A Christmas Orange

In the very early 1800s, a young boy about fourteen years old named John lived in an orphanage in Old England along with several other children. Orphanages were dreaded. "Orphan" meant unwanted and unloved. The orphanage was administered by a master and his wife who were results of meager backgrounds themselves and were short on love but high on discipline. No child-like play, no expression of compassion, no understanding.

Every day of the year was spent working. They worked in gardens, cleaned, sewed, and cooked sometimes for wealthy children. They were up at dawn and worked until dark and usually received only one meal a day. However, they were very grateful because they were taught to be hard workers. John had absolutely nothing to call his own. None of the children did.

Christmas was the one day of the year when the children did not work and received a gift. There was a gift for each child—something to call their own. This special gift was an orange. John had been in the orphanage long enough to look forward with delight and anticipation of this special day of Christmas and to the orange he would receive.

In Old England, and to John and his orphan companions, an orange was a rare and special gift. It had an unusual aroma of something they smelled only at Christmas. The children prized it so much that they kept it for several days, weeks, and even months—protecting it, smelling it, touching it, and loving it. Usually they tried to savor and preserve it for so long that it rotted before they ever peeled it to enjoy the sweet juice.

Many thoughts were expressed this year as Christmastime approached. The children would say, "I will keep mine the longest." They always talked about how big their last orange was and how long they had kept it. John usually slept with his next to his pillow. He would put it right by his nose and smell of its goodness, holding it tenderly and carefully as not to bruise it. He would dream of children all over the world smelling the sweet aroma of oranges. It gave him security and a sense of well-being, hope and dreams of a future filled with good food and a life different from this meager existence.

This year John was overjoyed by the Christmas season. He was becoming a man. He knew he was becoming stronger and soon he would be old enough to leave. He was excited by this anticipation and excited about Christmas. He would save his orange until his birthday in July. If he preserved it very carefully, kept it cool, and did not drop it, he might be able to eat it on his birthday.

Christmas Day finally came. The children were so excited as they entered the big dining hall. John could smell the unusual aroma of meat. In his excitement and because of his oversized feet, he tripped, causing a disturbance. Immediately the master roared, "John, leave the hall and there will be no orange for you this year." John's heart broke violently wide open. He began to cry. He turned and went swiftly back to the cold room and his corner so the small children would not see his anguish.

A little while later, he heard the door open, and each of the children entered. Little Elizabeth, with her hair falling over her shoulders, a smile on her face, and tears in her eyes, held out a piece of rag to John. "Here, John," she said, "this is for you." John was touched by her sweet and innocent face as he reached for the tiny package.

As he lifted back the edges of the rag, he saw a big juicy orange all peeled and quartered . . . and then he realized what they had done. Each had sacrificed their own orange by sharing a quarter and had created a big, beautiful orange for John.

John never forgot the sharing, love, and personal sacrifice his friends had shown him that Christmas Day. John's beginning was a meager existence; however, his growth to manhood was rewarded by wealth and success. In memory of that day, every year he would send oranges all over the world to children everywhere. His desire was that no child would ever spend Christmas without a special Christmas orange.

* pinecones sprayed silver or gold for tree ornaments
* "field and fountain, moor and mountain, following yonder star"
* children's expressions as they look at a manger scene
* china dolls:
  * little girl and boy babies
  * Victorian ladies
  * historic characters
* the smell of Mom's cherry pie baking
* opening presents in front of the fire with my sweetie
* Chinese checkers
* sharing the faith
* chocolate chips
* everyone reaching out to strangers
* choir robes
* "O Holy Night"
* choosing just one gift to open on Christmas Eve
* selecting Secret Santa names
* a red sunset above snow
* Christmas aprons
* the smell of bacon-and-egg omelets
* everyone saying, "Open mine next!"
* "five golden rings"
* kindness

* Christmas is an attitude of the heart to be celebrated every day
* throwing artificial icicles on the tree
* carefully hanging individual icicles on the tree

Christmas Jokes

What do snowmen eat for breakfast?
Snowflakes

There once was a czar in Russia whose name was Rudolph the Great. He was standing in his house one day with his wife. He looked out the window and saw something happening. He said to his wife, "Look honey. It's raining." She, being the obstinate type, responded, "I don't think so, dear. I think it's snowing." But Rudolph knew better. So he said to his wife, "Let's step outside and we'll find out." Lo and behold, they step outside and discover it was in fact rain. And Rudolph turns to his wife and replies, "I knew it was raining. Rudolph the Red knows rain, dear!"

* Christmas music piped into malls, over the office intercom, in elevators, subways, bus radios
* chubby cherub angel faces
* church craft fairs
* pines feathered with fresh snow
* baking bread for my neighbors
* Chutes 'N Ladders
* sharing talents with children
* "passing the peace" handshakes at our church
* old-fashioned oatmeal
* fan-shaped place cards
* a shepherd's leather bag
* cinnamon

What I like most about Christmas these days is reliving the enchanting season through my children's eyes. As we get older, we get so busy and so numb to the blessedness of Christmas. It's so nice to hear, "Wow! Baby Jesus was really born in a barn?"

LINDA ELLIOTT

SILENT NIGHT

Silent night! holy night!
All is calm, all is bright
round yon virgin mother and child,
Holy infant so tender and mild,
sleep in heavenly peace!
sleep in heavenly peace!

Silent night! holy night!
Shepherds quake at the sight;
glories stream from heaven afar,
heavenly hosts sing Alleluia,
Christ, the Saviour, is born!
Christ, the Saviour, is born!

Silent night! holy night!
Son of God, love's pure light
radiant beams from thy holy face,
with the dawn of redeeming grace,
Jesus, Lord at Thy birth.
Jesus, Lord at Thy birth.

JOSEPH MOHR

Traditions We Share with Our Church Family

* decorating the church together
* felt wall hangings made by the women's guild
* potluck dinners
* grandpas putting on reading glasses to sing from the hymnal
* moms with diaper bags
* the ushers
* the "shushers"
* boys throwing snowballs in the parking lot
* our choir forming a singing Christmas tree
* curls of smoke rising when the whole congregation blows out their candles

The thing I like most about Christmas is waiting for it. I try to put myself in shoes of the ancient Hebrews and wonder what it would be like to hear about this "Messiah" for so long ... and then when it happens, the triumph of expectation revealed in such a human/divine package. Of course I'd be skeptical. But then I imagine following his life, hearing the rumors, the wonder, the stories of this God-man, this Christ child, this Redeemer.

When Christmas day finally arrives, I begin a journey to Easter ... it's a never-ending cycle. Kind of the way our life in Christ is, a never-ending cycle; a celebration of all that is life and redeeming, so redeeming.

* pine-scented room spray
* cinnamon roasted almonds
* walking the mall to look at Christmas decorations
* clearing the dishes away together
* sharing popcorn with my honey at a romantic movie
* clothespin dolls
* cloverleaf rolls
* "Please bring a friend along!"
* kids that cry on Santa's lap
* old-fashioned glass tree ornaments:
  * German pickle
  * oranges
  * apples
  * gingerbread cottages
  * stars
  * angels
  * doves
  * birds with paintbrush feathers
  * squirrels
* Clue
* plaid skirts with woolly sweaters
* Cocoa Crispy treats
* Barbie's Dream House

* coffee cake:
  * cinnamon streusel
  * iced
  * chocolate swirled
  * date
  * raisin
  * cranberry
  * apple
  * apricot
* finding my lost mitten
* buying new mittens when I can't find my lost one
* Coke in a Santa can
* "power shopping" with the girls
* cold hands, warm hearts
* collapsing on the couch with my spouse after a day of "power shopping"
* homemade applesauce
* a cozy new hat that keeps your head warm and makes you look fashionable at the same time
* laughing with exhilaration into a cold winter wind
* having Christmas parties at school on the last day before vacation instead of doing school-work
* getting "Happy Christmas" cards from our friends in Ireland
* gathering in the kitchen before dinner for Grandpa's prayer over the whole extended family

O LITTLE TOWN OF BETHLEHEM

O little town of Bethlehem, how still we see thee lie!
Above thy deep and dreamless sleep the silent stars go by;
Yet in thy dark streets shineth the everlasting Light:
The hopes and fears of all the years
Are met in thee tonight.

How silently, how silently, the wondrous gift is given!
So God imparts to human hearts the blessing of His heaven.
No ear may hear His coming, but in this world of sin,
Where meek souls will receive Him still,
The dear Christ enters in.

PHILLIPS BROOKS

* flannel robes
* collecting Nativity scene figurines:
  * the baby Jesus
  * Mary kneeling in her blue robe
  * Joseph standing holding his staff
  * the wise men carrying gifts
  * shepherds holding lambs
  * angels with widespread wings
  * shopkeepers
  * peasants
  * bakers
  * horses
  * donkeys
  * sheep and lambs
  * birds
  * camels
* "Ready? Smile and say 'Merry Christmas!'"
* sharing our blessings with others
* a skating Christmas tree
* playing "steal the gift" with each other

* colorful jars of homemade preserves:
  * jellies
  * jams
  * pickles
  * watermelon
  * applesauce
  * corn
  * tomato paste
  * herb vinegar
  * mixed vegetables
* a shepherd's rustic blanket cape
* big, thirsty bath towels
* confetti candy sprinkles on cookie frosting
* oatmeal bread
* Constant Comment tea
  * Cozy Chamomile
  * Red Raspberry
  * Apple Cinnamon
* cookie cutters

A kid who doesn't believe Santa can get a million things in one bag ought to look inside his mother's purse!

Refreshment for the Season

❋ hot mulled cider with a cinnamon stick stir
❋ Hawaiian Punch in a coconut with a tiny paper umbrella
❋ Celestial Seasonings "Sleepy Time" tea
❋ cocoa in Styrofoam cups at the ice rink
❋ iced lemonade at the beach
❋ Maxwell House French roast coffee
❋ Cherry Coke
❋ tomato juice
❋ limeade
❋ twisty straws
❋ root beer floats
❋ sun tea

"When Christmas is over," said the merchant to the minister, "it's over, and it's our job to rid this store completely of Christmas in a day."

"Well," said the minister, "I've a bigger job—to keep Christmas in the hearts of people for a lifetime."

Eight Gifts That Don't Cost a Cent

THE GIFT OF LISTENING

But you must REALLY listen. No interruption, no day dreaming no planning your response. Just listening.

THE GIFT OF AFFECTION

Be generous with appropriate hugs, kisses, pats on the back and handholds. Let these small actions demonstrate the love you have for family and friends.

THE GIFT OF LAUGHTER

Clip cartoons. Share articles and funny stories. Your gift will say, "I love to laugh with you."

THE GIFT OF A WRITTEN NOTE

It can be a simple "Thanks for the help" note or a full sonnet. A brief, handwritten note may be remembered for a lifetime, and may even change a life.

THE GIFT OF A COMPLIMENT

A simple and sincere, "You look great in red," "You did a super job," or "That was a wonderful meal" can make someone's day.

THE GIFT OF A FAVOR

Every day, go out of your way to do something kind.

THE GIFT OF SOLITUDE

There are times when we want nothing better than to be left alone. Be sensitive to those times and give the gift of solitude to others.

THE GIFT OF A CHEERFUL DISPOSITION

The easiest way to feel good is to extend a kind word to someone, really it's not that hard to say, Hello or Thank you.

AUTHOR UNKNOWN

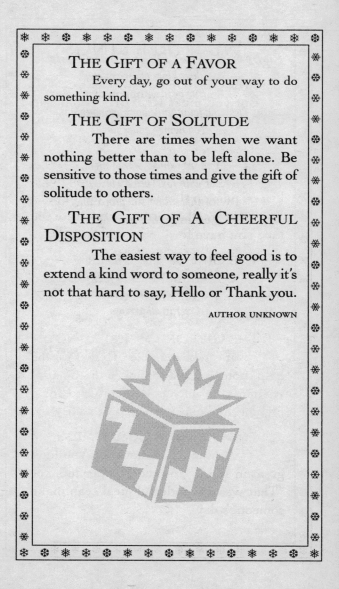

WE THREE KINGS

We three kings of Orient are;
Bearing gifts, we traverse afar,
Field and fountain, moor and mountain,
Following yonder star.

O star of wonder, star of night,
Star with royal beauty bright,
Westward leading, still proceeding,
Guide us to Thy perfect light.

Born a King on Bethlehem's plain,
Gold I bring to crown Him again,
King forever, ceasing never,
Over us all to reign.

JOHN HENRY HOPKINS

Easy Peanut Butter Fudge

1/4 C. peanut butter
1 stick of butter
1 box powdered sugar
1 Tsp. vanilla
milk for consistency

Melt 1/4 C. of peanut butter with 1 stick of butter. Add 1 box of powdered sugar and 1 tsp. vanilla. Add a little milk to make it easy to spread into a greased 9"x 13" glass baking dish. Chill until solid, cut and enjoy!

SUBMITTED BY KAREN SMITH

* Aunt Ruthie's Doberman statue wearing a red Santa cap
* Aunt Sandy's real Rotweiler wearing a red Santa cap
* corduroy slippers with plaid flannel lining
* corn bread stuffing
* counting our blessings
* kids playing under the dinner table
* serving plates with green stars around the edges
* not sitting by the table leg at Christmas dinner
* "seven swans a-swimming"
* hiding presents in the car trunk
* cows with steamy breath in the barn
* cracker and cheese platters: Swiss, Colby, Monterey Jack, American, pimento
* birdhouse Christmas tree ornaments
* nutmeg
* playing "guess what's in that package" on Christmas Eve
* a star to steer by
* Cracker Barrel restaurants
* progressive dinners
* progressive dinners that involve boating from house to house on a lake
* flannel sheets
* cranberries
* Cream of Wheat with a square of melting butter
* creating handmade Christmas cards

Every year it seems like my older brother Dustin gets more and more excited about Christmas morning and all of the presents he gets to open. We are hardly able to stop him from opening all of the presents beneath the tree before the exciting day! It was during the Christmas break of my sophomore year in college that it seemed like he was more excited then ever. I was pretty tired from finals so getting out of bed was not fun. After trying many times to get me up Dustin took matters into his own hands, and promptly grabbed my foot and dragged me down the stairs so that we could get to opening presents.

HEIDI CARVELLA

What do Eskimos buy at Christmas time?
    Christmas Seals

- crepes sprinkled with cinnamon and sugar
- crewelwork doilies
- croissant rolls for breakfast
- Cross pen sets
- seashell angel ornaments with coquina wings, scallop shell gowns, button shell hats
- crystal angel earrings
- new snow on Christmas Eve
- Norman Rockwell moments
- crystal goblets with your initials engraved on them
- cuddling on an overstuffed couch to watch "It's a Wonderful Life"
- curly elf shoes

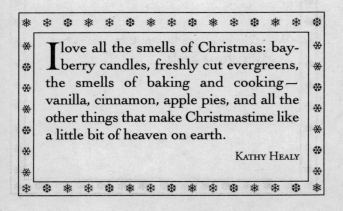

I love all the smells of Christmas: bayberry candles, freshly cut evergreens, the smells of baking and cooking—vanilla, cinnamon, apple pies, and all the other things that make Christmastime like a little bit of heaven on earth.

KATHY HEALY

What I like about Christmas is the spirit of unselfishness that we seem to have as we focus on our Lord and Savior's birth. Each Christmas Eve my husband brings our children to the local food kitchen with an abundance of toys that are no longer played with in our household. They receive new toys at Christmas, and we encourage them to go through their belongings the week before Christmas and decide which things are in good enough condition that they could pass them on to someone who may not have much. The toys are then distributed to the children at the food kitchen when they have their Christmas dinner; also, when possible I bake batches of homemade cookies to be given out. Yes, the children there receive a gift that may bring a smile to their face and their parents' face, but we are the ones who receive the blessing. The saying is true: "In giving we receive!"

Special Christmas blessings our family has enjoyed:

_____

_____

_____

_____

_____

_____

_____

_____

_____

_____

_____

_____

_____

_____

❋ playing Santa at the housing project
❋ Currier and Ives
❋ customized computer Christmas cards
❋ cute paper napkin prints
❋ cut-out snowflakes in windows
❋ assembling all the toys
❋ having the toys assembled by the store
❋ "six geese a-laying"
❋ scented oil lamps
❋ fleecy snow clouds
❋ kids in new Christmas jammies
❋ new puppy meeting new kitten
❋ Dad asking if we are going to sleep all day
❋ dancers dressed like nutcracker soldiers
❋ dancing together by the Christmas tree after
   the kids are in bed
❋ date pudding
❋ smiling back at strangers who say hello
❋ deciding how to display our lighting collection
❋ Santa's Workshop at the foot of Pike's Peak
❋ decorating my college dorm with my hallmates
   while singing carols at the top of our lungs
❋ folding the wrapping paper to save
❋ Nativity scenes in store windows
❋ blue spruce Christmas trees
❋ decorating the fireplace mantel

One of my favorite Christmas traditions is playing "pass the present" to the story of "Twas the Night before Christmas." We buy "generic" presents and pass them out to each person in a circle. Then the story is read and when you hear certain words such as a body part or an animal, you have to pass your present to the person to the right or to the left of you.

JUDY SEXTON

I do come home at Christmas. We all do, or we all should. We all come home, or ought to come home, for a short holiday—the longer, the better—from the great boarding school where we are forever working at our arithmetical slates, to take, and give a rest.

CHARLES DICKENS

O COME ALL YE FAITHFUL

O come, all ye faithful,
Joyful and triumphant,
Oh come ye, O come ye to Bethlehem;
Come and behold Him,
Born the King of angels;
O come, let us adore Him,
O come, let us adore Him,
O come, let us adore Him,
Christ the Lord.
Sing, choirs of angels,
Sing in exultation,
Sing, all ye citizens of heaven above;
Glory to God
In the highest:
O come, let us adore Him,
O come, let us adore Him,
O come, let us adore Him,
Christ the Lord.

TRADITIONAL HYMN,
TRANSLATED FROM LATIN BY F. OAKELEY

* blinking tree lights
* non-blinking tree lights
* decorative stamps on the back of envelopes
* deer with their babies grazing in the moonlight at our feeder
* kids holding up sippy cups
* Dickens' *A Christmas Carol*
* folks are more patient with each other
* dining out with just the two of us
* Disney ornaments:
  * Minnie and Mickey
  * Pluto
  * Goofy
  * Donald Duck
  * Chip and Dale
  * Cinderella
  * Snow White and the Seven Dwarves
  * Sleeping Beauty
  * Alice in Wonderland and the Cheshire Cat
* blueberry pancakes
* Santa's wonderland at the mall
* The song "Breath of Heaven"
* Grace College's Christmas program "Light of His Coming"

* a stocking stuffed with:
  * favorite music CDs
  * computer games
  * wooden puzzle games
  * fishing tackle
  * hand lotions
  * scented soap
  * coffee samplers
  * tea assortments
  * baseball cards
  * Star Wars toys
  * old-fashioned metal toys
  * wooden blocks
  * stuffed animals
  * dominoes
  * jacks
  * bubble soap and wands
  * bubble bath packages
  * tiny gift books
  * bookmarks
  * a new watch
  * shaving gel
  * a devotional book
  * Hot Wheels cars
  * candles
  * a quill pen
  * a mini picture frame
* the love of God as our focus
* "sleep in heavenly peace"
* dog choir barking "Jingle Bells"

* dollhouse furnishings:
  * little couches
  * tables
  * Christmas trees
  * beds with quilts
  * rocking chairs
  * baby cradles
  * kitchen sinks
  * tiny candles
  * clothes hangers with clothes
  * mirrors
  * tiny framed pictures
  * ceramic people

Time was with most of us, when Christmas Day, encircling all our limited world like a magic ring, left nothing out for us to miss or seek; bound together all our home enjoyments, affections, and hopes; grouped everything and everyone round the Christmas fire, and make the little picture shining in our bright young eyes, complete.

CHARLES DICKENS

❋ wooden nutcracker dolls: soldiers, Santas, Uncle Sam, animals
❋ my grandparents' Christmas stories from the old country
❋ boot prints of various sizes
❋ dominoes
❋ hanging wreaths and garlands together
❋ French toast for breakfast
❋ door prizes at Christmas parties
❋ saying hello to strangers and having them smile back
❋ blue-eyed kittens
❋ doorbell chimes
❋ Douglas fir Christmas trees
❋ dressing up as Christmas characters for a photo: Nativity scene, Victorian carolers, elves, reindeer
❋ a time to start over again
❋ my grandpa's secret recipe for snow ice cream
❋ dried-flower arrangements:
  ❋ roses
  ❋ holly
  ❋ baby's breath
  ❋ yarrow
  ❋ sedum
  ❋ eucalyptus branches

* drinking from the good china teacups with saucers
* "Sleigh Ride"
* fresh Christmas tree lots
* bread pans
* the light of one candle in the darkness
* pressed-flower stationary
* driving around with my family to see the Christmas lights
* eating hot and gooey orange Danish rolls before opening presents on Christmas morning
* a trail of hidden messages throughout the house that leads you to a wonderful present
* "The Little Tin Soldier"
* Worchestershire sauce
* Trying to pronounce Worchestershire sauce
* buying calendars at 50% off the week after Christmas

Neighbors and Neighborhoods

* the church parking lot traffic volunteers
* honking horns to greet neighbors (instead of for less positive reasons!)
* your neighbor's driveway filled with cars
* your own driveway filled with cars
* the holiday home tour

* my Grandma's special chocolate pie
* handwritten Christmas letters
* Ebenezer Scrooge
* kids dressed like reindeer in a parade
* "so bring Him incense, gold, and myrrh"
* fresh green wreaths
* echoes of angels' songs in the night

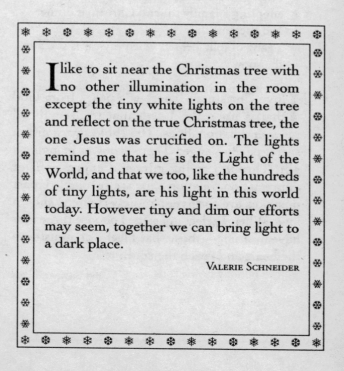

I like to sit near the Christmas tree with no other illumination in the room except the tiny white lights on the tree and reflect on the true Christmas tree, the one Jesus was crucified on. The lights remind me that he is the Light of the World, and that we too, like the hundreds of tiny lights, are his light in this world today. However tiny and dim our efforts may seem, together we can bring light to a dark place.

VALERIE SCHNEIDER

Reaching Out to Others

* giving toys to a church nursery
* a Marine at Toys-for-Tots
* making a snow dragon with the neighborhood children
* hot chocolate and spiced cider for our guests in Florida
* washing cars in the hot California sun as a Christmas charity fund raiser
* buying gifts for the "Angel Tree"
* adopting a family to send Christmas dinner and presents to
* a gang of jolly helpers when my car is stuck in the snow

I love Christmas. There is a peace from God that is upon the Earth that transcends all races and nationalities. The Bible says a gift in secret pacifies anger. There is power in giving a gift. Through giving gifts and expressions of appreciation, relationships are reconciled, past mistakes are forgiven, and everyone is shown love. When I select my gifts, I choose those that have meaning—those that I feel will minister to the heart and reach the soul.

BEVERLY MEADOWS

❋ eclectic assortment of chairs from every room squeezed around the big table

❋ edible decorations to hang on our Christmas tree

❋ eggnog with nutmeg sprinkled on top

❋ "Son of God, love's pure light"

❋ electric blankets

❋ my first Christmas ornament

❋ keepsake ornaments handed down from my grandmother

❋ a tiny babe wrapped in a blanket

❋ elves in green shoes

❋ fresh squeezed orange juice

❋ e-mail Christmas greetings

❋ hand-sewn felt ornaments

❋ "songs of good cheer, Christmas is here"

❋ English muffins

❋ getting an engagement ring for Christmas

❋ giving an engagement ring for Christmas

❋ entertaining angels unaware

❋ a Victorian dollhouse under the tree

❋ Santa's little wooden house on the lawn of the courthouse

❋ erasable message boards: outside the door, by the phone, on the fridge

❋ the light of Christ

❋ errands of love

❋ bread pudding

Christmas in Sweden

In Sweden, the eldest daughter in a family wears an evergreen wreath with candles on her head and serves coffee and buns to her family for breakfast on Dec. 13. This ritual remembers St. Lucia who carried food to the early Christians hiding from persecution in dark underground tunnels. To light the way, she wore a wreath of candles on her head.

Bring a torch, Jeanette, Isabella
Bring a torch, come swiftly and run.
Christ is born, tell the folk of the village,
Jesus is sleeping in His cradle,
Ah, ah, beautiful is the Mother,
Ah, ah, beautiful is her Son.

TRANSLATED BY E. CUTHBERT NUNN

* espresso:
  * petite
  * medium
  * stay-awake-all-night sizes
* everyone is nice to each other
* faces of little kids at our bedside, waiting for us to wake up
* faith
* fake snow from a can
* musical jewelry boxes
* a white porcelain manger scene
* falling asleep in the car with my cheek on the fur collar of Grandma's coat
* falling asleep reading Dr. Seuss to the kids
* familiar handwriting on the Christmas cards from our mailbox
* family photos on the mantel
* fancy lace tablecloths
* wooden rocking horse
* white fur muffs
* brightly colored envelopes in the mailbox
* Father Christmas
* favorite Christmas records, tapes and CDs
* feeling too full to get up from the table
* felt stocking-shaped placemats
* "star of wonder, star of night, star with royal beauty bright"

* Fentonware:
  * candy dishes
  * kitten figures
  * lamps
  * vases
* festive jewelry:
  * Christmas bulb earrings
  * reindeer broaches
  * snowflake necklaces
  * Santa pins
  * snowman earrings
  * jingle bell necklaces
* finding that perfect black velvet dress for your fancy Christmas dinner party
* gathering for Christmas with my husband's family at Camp Luz: sleeping in bunk beds, singing around the lodge house fire, pulling together all the available tables and crowding the whole family around for Christmas dinner
* avoiding getting that "bug" that's going around
* being pregnant at Christmas time
* Radio City Music Hall's Christmas Extravaganza
* getting a good back rub after shoveling snow
* getting a good foot rub after shopping all day

* Mom whispering Christmas present secrets to Grandma on the phone
* jingle bells on doorways
* fifties car ornaments
* brown-and-serve rolls
* hand-painted scarves
* "The Grinch Who Stole Christmas" cartoon
* Fig Newtons
* filled chocolate creams:
  * orange
  * pineapple
  * vanilla
  * raspberry
* green vestments
* finally finding that gift you looked all over for
* "Stay up as late as you like; I'm going to bed."
* Santa skiing in a red wet suit
* fireworks on Christmas Eve
* flannel boxer shorts
* catching Mommy kissing Santa
* catching Santa kissing Mommy
* fleece loungewear
* floating candles
* model train cars: the black train engine, the red caboose, coal cars, cattle cars, sleeper cars, lumber flats
* folding chairs
* Folger's Colombian coffee
* green palm trees strung with Christmas lights
* folk tales

Legend of the Shepherd Boy and the Wreath

A poor boy had no gift to give the Holy Child, so he made a tiny crown of leaves from a Holly Bush. Compared to the expensive gifts that the others had given, the crown seeded of little value, so the little shepherd boy began to cry as he presented it. But when the Babe touched the Holly crown with His tiny hand, the leaves suddenly gleamed and the teardrops turned to scarlet berries.

Through the centuries the Holly wreath became a traditional Christmas decoration, reminding us of the Miracle of Christ's Birth.

* fondue: Swiss, cheddar, chocolate
* brown-eyed puppies with red bows
* "ten lords a-leaping"
* the golden crowns of the wise men
* Santa lollipops
* Franciscan stoneware
* frankincense and myrrh, the gifts of holiness
* Franklin stoves
* white gloves on little girls
* mint melt-aways
* French bread
* fresh Christmas fruit:
    * oranges
    * pomegranates
    * apples
    * grapefruit
    * red and yellow pears
    * kiwi
    * star fruit
* friendly Ping-Pong tournaments
* green cat eyes shining under the couch
* "The Carol of the Bells"
* candles, the symbol for Jesus, the Light of the World
* fringed holiday table runners
* Frost's "Stopping by Woods on a Snowy Evening"

* white, green, red, or pink icing on Christmas
  cookies
* Russian snowballs
* brownies baking
* frosted spruce needles
* mint jelly
* salespeople who wrap purchases in tissue paper
* "Joseph's Song" by Michael Card
* "Mary, Did You Know" by Mark Lowry
* a big snow drift that covers your backyard fence
  so you can walk right overtop of the fence and
  into the yard
* watching a cat walk in snow (shaking each paw
  with every step)

I am so glad each Christmas Eve,
The night of Jesus' birth!
Then like the sun the star shone forth,
And angels sang on earth.

The little Child in Bethlehem,
He was a King indeed!
For He came down from Heaven above
To help a world in need.

INGER MARIE LYCKE WEXELSEN

I enjoy the Christmas string tradition — I think this is a tradition that began in France. There's a story about a widow who would always give children toys at Christmas. One Christmas she was so poor that after she had bought presents for all the kids in the village, she didn't have any money to buy ornaments for her tree. So, she put string on her tree as decoration. The story goes that the next morning when she woke up, the Christ Child had come and blessed her generosity by replacing the string with strands of real silver and gold. The tradition is to put string on the tree and then replace it with silver and gold garland on Christmas Eve, so that when the children get up in the morning they see the silver and gold strands. Then you read the Christmas story from the Bible together as a family.

JUDY SEXTON

* Frosty the Snowman:
  * carrot nose
  * black coal eyes
  * sticks for hands
  * old galoshes
  * black top hat
  * yarn for hair
  * a plaid wool scarf
* candy canes for the Sunday school class
* frozen puddles
* electronic Christmas cards that play music
* Christmas cards that don't play music
* Grandpa's favorite sweater
* the golden color of straw in the manger
* fruit-flavored candy canes
* furry Santa Claus hats
* fuzzy earmuffs
* Gabriel's announcement to Mary
* "The Carol of the Friendly Beasts"
* Candyland
* garlands of green pine around the sanctuary
* rosy red cheeks of little kids outside
* gas logs
* gathered puffball comforters
* miniature ponies peeking through the fence
* generous giving

A three year old once gave this reaction to her Christmas dinner: "I don't like the turkey, but I like the bread he ate."

B usinessmen are saying that this could be the greatest Christmas ever. I always thought that the first one was.

ART FETTING

W ith every recurring Christmas morning the prospects of the world's peace grow brighter, and the practice of universal brotherhood comes a little nearer to the door.

ANONYMOUS

Christmas with Grandma and Grandpa

❋ Grandpa's attic:
  ❋ old cedar chests and big black trunks
  ❋ racks of clothes that smell like mothballs
  ❋ old books in boxes
  ❋ a bare light bulb with a pull chain
  ❋ Grandma's wedding dress
  ❋ Grandpa's military uniform
  ❋ reels of home movies
  ❋ boxes of postcards, photos, and letters
  ❋ big funny hats
  ❋ someone's old snowshoes
  ❋ a mounted deer head
  ❋ Life magazines
❋ helping Granddad check the bulbs on his homemade Christmas wreaths
❋ Grandma carrying her famous Christmas ham into the dining room as we all say, "Ahhh!"
❋ a bubble bath in Grandma's big, old-fashioned claw-foot bathtub
❋ when Grandma says, "Now you go sit down while I make coffee."
❋ how even the boring details of your life are interesting to Granny and Granddad
❋ Grandma and Granddad getting to know a new great-grandchild

* all the cute name variations the grandchildren use to say "Grandma and Grandpa":
  * Nonna
  * Aba
  * Gamma
  * Gapa
  * Poppa
  * Dandan
  * Mamaw
  * Baba
* my grandpa saying, "My grandkids aren't spoiled; all babies smell like that!"
* just the right number of quarters in Grandpa's pocket for the grandkids
* Grandma's special treasure chest with old-fashioned clothes in which the children play dress-up
* how my grandma thought she knew just what her little dog wanted to say
* how my grandma and grandpa tell each other they are wrong all the time, and still end up agreeing about everything
* my grandparents' tradition of giving each grandchild a silver Christmas coin with their name and the year engraved on it

Christmas in Spain

The children of Spain leave their shoes on the windowsills filled with straw, carrots, and barley for the horses of the Wise Men, who they believe reenact their journey to Bethlehem every year. One of the wise men is called Balthazar, who leaves the children gifts. They call Christmas Eve Nochebuena, and families gather together to rejoice and share a meal around the Nativity scene.

* getting a bargain at a hotel
* giant color swirl lollipops
* rosemary
* gift box of:
    * scarves
    * glove and hat set
    * stockings
    * bath salts
    * fancy soaps
    * jellies
    * assorted earrings
    * ChapStick
    * monogrammed handkerchiefs
    * note cards
    * sunglasses and SPF lotion
* gingerbread
* "The First Noel"
* Girl Scouts making Christmas ornaments
* giving
* a toddler's great big yawn
* Mom trying to politely hide a yawn
* giving my best guy the sweater I pictured him in
* gloves with fur cuffs
* God working miracles in the hearts of people
* going through old family photo albums together

* gold angel decorations
* rose petals and "I love you" written on snow
* babies playing peek-a-boo
* good food and good company
* goose down comforters and pillows
* Granddad chopping wood for the Christmas hearth
* foreign exchange students over for Christmas break
* getting invited to a family's home for Christmas when I was a foreign exchange student
* Christmas dinner
* grandparents waiting by the front door for us to arrive
* grandparents waving good-bye from the front porch until we are out of sight
* gray kittens with pink ribbons
* great golden angel wings
* watching for the mail truck
* green as a symbol for God's gift of everlasting life and hope
* rocking horses and cowboy hats
* Gummy Bears
* Gund stuffed animals
* "The anticipation of waiting for Christmas, just as the Hebrews waited for the Messiah."
* carolers' red noses
* handbell choirs playing carols

* white-and-red-striped dishcloths
* Handel's Messiah
* hand-knit Christmas stockings
* hanging strings of popcorn on the Christmas tree
* hash browns with ketchup
* Haviland china place setting
* having a Secret Santa
* warming my fingers around a cup of hot chocolate
* hayride at the tree farm
* hazelnut coffee with whipped cream and nutmeg on top
* a college care package for Christmas:
  * laundry detergent
  * many rolls of quarters
  * caramel popcorn in a plastic tub
  * a box of chewy fruit snacks
  * a prepaid phone card
  * a jar of mixed nuts
  * a package of new ink pens
  * envelopes with stamps already on them
* handmade stockings
* my dad reciting "'Twas the Night Before Christmas" to us from memory

The Son of God
became man
to enable men to become
the sons of God.

C. S. LEWIS

* "The Gift of the Magi"
* a children's choir
* red-tailed hawks soaring
* hearing the drip of icicles melting outside
* heirloom quilts
* the glow of white lights on tall trees outdoors
* helping Grandma get out her best china for Christmas dinner
* herb shops
* Hershey's miniatures
* hiding gifts so the kids won't find them before Christmas
* his and hers pajama set
* carols played by a brass quintet
* puppy waiting under the dining table for crumbs
* His special star
* "The Legend of the Sand Dollar" on a mug
* the first snowflake falling
* red spiral candles
* home
* wrapping presents at the last minute
* getting out all the presents I've wrapped ahead of time
* getting to spend Christmas with your boyfriend who lives 11 hours away
* putting pennies in your new penny loafers
* streusel-topped pear pie

* Hummel figurines:
  * little girl with umbrella
  * little boys
  * grandparents
  * pets
* hope
* horehound candy
* hot chocolate with marshmallows
* how children always have room for Christmas dessert

I love the way my little brother is always so delighted about Christmas, even if he is covered with marker and chicken pox scabs.

KATIE BOTKIN

I love the celebration of Jesus Christ. His spirit is so alive and so close at Christmastime. It's all around us. It's wonderful!

LAURA ANNE LORD

Every day should be Christmas in the hearts of all Christians. Spread joy, goodwill and the Word 365 days a year!

REVEREND J. D. PATTERSON

Christmas in the Country

* the cider press at the apple farm
* trees with frosted branches that look as if they are sugar glazed
* Jack Frost nipping at your nose
* warming barrels by skating ponds
* rabbit tracks in the snow
* a maple sugaring house in Vermont
* needing sunglasses because of "snowshine"
* needing sunglasses for the beach

I love the snow-filled arms of evergreens. I love crisp, fresh snowflakes pirouetting like ballerinas in the breeze. Even while living in southern California sans snow, I loved the magic of Christmas. I love driving on Candy Tree Lane, where blocks of homes display fantastic sights of countless lights and reindeer and Nativity scenes.

MARGARET JOHNSON

❋ how eager children are for you to try to guess their Christmas secrets

❋ the way Grandma is sure children will "catch their death of cold" out in the snow

❋ when my little niece yells, "Ouch!" when she touches the prickly pine branch

❋ "the world in solemn stillness lay to hear the angels sing"

❋ red rubber noses that make you look like Rudolph

❋ the bright stars in the still night

❋ my sweetie buys me everything two sizes smaller than I really am

❋ "The Twelve Days of Christmas"

❋ how tickled my wife is to surprise me with a gift

❋ huge Christmas trees in fancy hotel lobbies

❋ hugs

❋ hurricane lamps

❋ iced sugar cookie cutouts: Santa, reindeer, Christmas trees, bears, stars, hearts

❋ icicle light sets

❋ a chance meeting on the street

❋ a former teacher

❋ "Come again soon!"

❋ "Nice to see you again!"

❋ "My, how you've grown!"

❋ "You look just the same as in high school!"

At Christmas play and make good cheer,
For Christmas comes but once a year.

THOMAS TUSSER

God rest ye merry gentlemen,
Let nothing you dismay;
Remember Christ our Savior,
Was born on Christmas Day.

TRADITIONAL CAROL

Heap on more wood!-the wind is chill;
But let it whistle as it will,
We'll keep our Christmas merry still.

SIR WALTER SCOTT

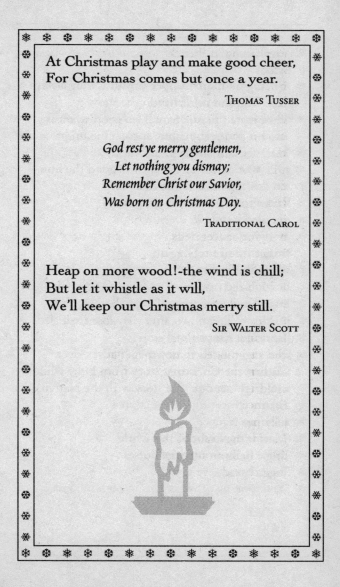

* carols sung in French
* igloos
* when grandparents open any gift, they always say, "You shouldn't have!"
* illuminated plastic Santas on people's roofs
* instant oatmeal: maple, apple, cinnamon, raisin
* Internet Christmas photo sites
* "It's Wonderful Life" is just as good the hundredth time as it is the first
* Jack Frost Mountain's ski trails
* the sledding hill:
    * flying saucer sleds
    * family-size toboggans
    * Radio Flyers
    * high-tech racers
    * inflated inner tubes
    * kids rolling down after they lose their sleds
* James Herriot animal stories
* cheerful models in newspaper ads
* reading the Christmas story from Luke while children "act out" the story with the Nativity figures
* jelly jars
* Jesus is the Light of the World
* jingle bells on carriage horses
* Jogga bread

❄ "there's a song in the air, there's a star in the sky"
❄ the baking aisle at the grocery store:
    ❄ powdered sugar
    ❄ unbleached flour
    ❄ brown sugar
    ❄ cream of tartar
    ❄ Crisco shortening
    ❄ olive oil
    ❄ Red Star yeast
❄ bib ski pants
❄ lying in bed on a blustery snowy night, listening to the wind howl, and feeling all snuggly in your own bed
❄ all the goodies that come from vendors to our office:
    ❄ shrimp cocktail
    ❄ chocolate and nut covered apples
    ❄ Toblerone oranges
    ❄ fudge in every flavor
    ❄ Harry and David fruit baskets
❄ graduating from college a semester early so you're done by Christmas time
❄ finding relatives at the airport when they come for the holidays
❄ my five-year-old daughter dancing in her department store tutu as the Nutcracker is shown on TV
❄ Johnson's Baby Oil

Soon after my sister-in-law and her boyfriend became engaged his doctor discovered a cancerous lump on his lung. Although their first year of marriage was a blur of radiation and chemotherapy, at the end of the treatments, Chris was given a clean bill of health. We all thought of our tearful prayer over him during our Christmas gathering just a few months before and rejoiced

Around Thanksgiving of their second year of marriage, Chris discovered a lump on his neck. The cancer had returned. He would begin treatment again immediately. We were all sad to learn that they would not be able to make the trip from California to Ohio for Christmas, but we understood.

As my husband and I drove to Cincinnati for his family's Christmas that year, we talked of Fran and Chris and sighed over the fact that we would not see them this year. We arrived at his brother Linford's house at dusk and began unloading all our luggage and many, many gifts. As we walked in the door we were greeted by my husband's many siblings, nieces, nephews, friendly dogs and immediately my eyes met with those of Chris and Fran. They had made it and surprised us.

My husband continued to greet his family and I quickly realized that he hadn't seen his sister and her husband standing right in front of him. The look on his face when he did finally see them was priceless. He stood shocked for a moment and then rushed to embrace them both.

We enjoyed a wonderful visit with the entire family, but especially with Chris and Fran. Chris' hopeful outlook in the face of another round of treatment was an inspiration and encouragement to us all.

We will always remember that one special Christmas surprise when God blessed us with another holiday all together, and we continue to rejoice, for now, nearly two years later, Chris is once again healthy and he and Fran are enjoying a full life together in their California home.

MOLLY DETWEILER

In our house we have begun a tradition where we draw names from within our immediate family. Each person is expected to make or give a gift that shows love for the person whose name they drew.

The rule is, you can't go to the store and buy anything. We did this for the first time last year. My husband and I have three children, at that time ages seven, four, and two months. My husband cried when he unwrapped an ornament our seven-year-old son had spent hours putting together. It wouldn't have sold for much at the store, but he had a reason for every little decoration he put on it.

When the kids understand gifts are a celebration of Jesus' sacrifice, Christmas is a powerful and moving holiday full of joy and love. It comes in December but is really the beginning of our year, of our hope.

MELINDA McINNIS

Christmas Crafts

* iron-on t-shirt decals
* clothespin reindeer ornaments
* button dolls
* needlepoint handbags
* wooden bead necklaces
* sweatshirts with puff-paint decorations

I love Christmas because it gives me a reason and excuse to indulge my family with wonderful, exciting gifts and foods that I would hesitate to spoil them with any other time. I love their faces and exuberance as we spend the entire day together. I love the smells, the colors, and the cold on my nose. I love the music, piped through the intercoms in all the stores. I love the way, for those weeks in time, Jesus is the focus of things, and no one can put you off for talking about him. I adore Christmas.

JR. MANZ

* someone offering an arm to help me out of the car
* kittens crowding in around a bowl of milk
* a jolly crowd at the dinner table
* a quiet dinner table for two
* knitted and crocheted gifts: scarves, hats, mittens, blankets and throws, slippers
* Kool-Aid slurpies
* kruscheki
* telling the children the "Night before Christmas" poem
* "this is Christ the King, whom shepherds guard and angels sing"
* lace handkerchief angel ornaments
* lambs and sheep
* lampposts glowing down cobblestone streets
* late Christmas cards-even after New Year's
* waking up to sleigh bells jingling
* Latin oratorios
* laughter in the malls
* cheese soufflé
* talking with my prayer partner
* La-Z-Boy recliners
* leaving a gift in our mailbox for the mailman
* "three French hens"
* sunflower seeds
* Lefton china teacups

I have always thought of Christmas time when it comes round, as a good time; a kind, forgiving, charitable time; the only time I know of, in the long calendar of the year, when men and women seem by one consent to open their shut-up hearts freely, and to think of people below them as if they were fellow passengers ... and not another race of creatures bound on other journeys.... And so as Tiny Tim said: "A merry Christmas to us all, my dears. God bless us, every one."

CHARLES DICKENS

It is Christmas in the mansion,
    Yule-log fires and silken frocks;
It is Christmas in the cottage,
    Mother's filling little socks.
It is Christmas on the highway,
    In the thronging, busy mart;
But the dearest, truest Christmas
    Is the Christmas in the heart.

ANONYMOUS

* Legos
* lemon cookies
* Lenox Christmas dishes
* licking the icing bowl
* licorice
* sugared pecans
* waking up on Christmas morning and thinking, "It's Jesus' birthday!"
* Lifesavers Christmas books
* light filtering through frosted windowpanes
* lighthouse ornaments
* Lincoln Logs
* stuffed animals with red ribbons
* linen napkins
* Linus' blanket as a shepherd's cape
* remembering a friend on my Christmas card list that I hadn't written to all year
* being remembered by a friend on my Christmas card list that I hadn't written to all year
* listening to Christmas music as we string lights
* little boys in red suit coats
* "two turtle doves"
* chenille robes
* stuffed draft stoppers propped against the doors
* tiny cherub wings

* cozy, little Christmas shops in the mall, full of glittering ornaments
* a gigantic fresh Christmas tree
* trying to get a gigantic fresh Christmas tree through the door
* steamed-up kitchen windows
* "we three kings of Orient are; bearing gifts, we traverse afar"
* cherry baked ham
* little kids dragging their favorite stuffed animal
* liturgical dance
* quilted vests
* sticky pecan rolls
* llamas with woven hiking packs
* looking at the stars
* Lorna Doone cookies

What I like about Christmas is the special feeling that it gives to us, whether excitement or anticipation, warmth, or closeness to family. It somehow feels like a renewal of hope, which is exactly what our Savior gives to us.

JANICE WATTS

The Story of Silent Night

The young priest was worried. Within 24 hours he was supposed to lead a Christmas Eve service, but he had no music. The Salzach River that flowed near the village church of Oberndorf, Austria, caused chronic moisture which had rusted the pipe organ. Without the organ there would be no music. And what was Christmas Eve without music?

Father Josef Mohr had but recently come to this tiny village. The night of December 23 he had attended the town Christmas play. But instead of going home afterwards, he had climbed the small mountain overlooking the town and soaked in the beauty and quiet of the darkness. It was nearly midnight before he reached his room. And so in the wee hours of December 24, 1818, he sat down to pen a new song, one which could be played on a guitar-at least that wasn't broken.

"Stille Nacht! Heilige Nacht!" he wrote. "Silent night, holy night." The nighttime peacefulness of Oberndorf was fresh in his mind; beyond it he could imagine Bethlehem, bathed in moonglow:

All is calm, all is bright.
Round yon Virgin Mother and child!
Holy Infant so tender and mild,
Sleep in heavenly peace.

The words were flowing now. He could visualize shepherds quaking, shaken from the quietness of their vigil by the glories streaming from heaven. He could see the child's countenance:

Son of God, love's pure light,
Radiant beams from Thy holy face
With the dawn of redeeming grace,
Jesus, Lord, at Thy birth.

It wasn't long 'til the simple poem was finished. Now, perhaps he could sleep.

The next morning he brought the poem to his organist, Franz Grüber. "I know it's the last minute," he must have said, "but could you put a tune to this song for the service tonight? Something simple that I could accompany on the guitar?" Father Mohr was new to the parish, and to the church's chief musician. But then, Grüber was being paid, and at that moment his beloved organ wouldn't work. Grüber set about the task quickly and in a couple of hours he was done, just in time to rehearse with the choir before the service. Mohr sang tenor, Grüber sang bass, and the service went off beautifully with the new song. "Stille Nacht! Heilige Nacht!"

A master organ builder eventually came to Oberndorf to repair the rusted organ, and there learned of the carol. He copied the song and doubtless sang it as he worked on organs in the neighboring villages. From him, two families of traveling folk singers, similar to the Trapp Family Singers of "Sound of Music" fame, learned of the song and sang it in concerts all over Europe. In 1834 the Strasser family performed it for the king of Prussia, who ordered it sung every Christmas Eve by his cathedral choir. The Rainer family singers brought it to America in 1839.

Sometimes the smallest churches make the biggest contributions. In this case, God presented a most wonderful carol to the world from a tiny congregation, one that just happened to be called St. Nicholas' Church of Oberndorf.

Christmas is for Kids . . . of All Ages

* how amazed children are that Daddy and Mommy were once little too
* toddlers kissing under the mistletoe
* helping children put on a Christmas play
* playing with children and all their new toys
* a toddler tasting the snow on his glove
* playing guessing games with children about that mysterious box under the tree
* our little boy concentrating so carefully to hold his Christmas candle straight up at church
* a little boy in a suit and clip-on tie
* toddlers saying, "More pleeese!"

It is good to be children sometimes, and never better than at Christmas, when its mighty Founder was a child Himself.

CHARLES DICKENS

* lots of free time to downhill ski, cross-country ski, water-ski, swim, hike, boat, surf, bike, go snowmobiling, play volleyball and tennis, make ice sculptures, snowshoe, sled
* walking out to get the mail and wondering what will be there
* staying in a posh hotel
* Louisiana gumbo
* babies in shopping cart seats
* love
* luminaria
* waking up because people are whispering so as not to wake you
* "We Three Kings"
* cherry crisp
* lyrics children make up to carols
* Maine lobster
* majestic faces on angels
* making bread by hand
* manger scene window clings
* maple sugar syrup
* Mark Twain anthologies
* Victorian carriages
* Mary's blue robe
* stained-glass windows
* Matchbox car garage and car wash
* McDonald's eggnog shakes and gift certificates
* meeting all my sweetheart's family
* "What Child Is This?"

* memories that spring from ornaments I received each year as a child
* children explaining the real meaning of Christmas
* waking when someone rings the doorbell
* men sitting outside stores waiting and waiting and waiting ...
* meringue star cookies
* messages on the answering machine
* Mexican tea cakes
* stained-glass window candy
* waking to the sound of someone humming a carol
* milk shake glasses and spoons
* baking cookies that look like Christmas trees
* eating cookies that look like Christmas trees
* "What's this in the bottom of my stocking?"
* miniature Nativity countrysides: hills made from sand, silk palm trees, cotton ball clouds, streams made from aluminum foil
* children falling asleep in Grandpa's lap

There's a song in the air!
There's a star in the sky!
There's a mother's deep prayer
    And a Baby's low cry!
And the star rains its fire where the
    Beautiful sing
For the manger of Bethlehem
    cradles a King.

JOSIAH GILBERT HOLLAND

This is how God showed his love among us: He sent his one and only Son into the world that we might live through him.

1 JOHN 4:9

* mint ice cream stars
* "Miracle on 34th Street"
* mittens with fur cuffs
* model Christmas villages:
  * skating figures on mirror ponds
  * quaint shops
  * horses and carriages
  * barns
  * miniature trees
  * tiny sidewalks
  * fences and street signs
  * bridges
* vanilla hand lotion
* Mom and Dad tucking us in
* stained-glass Tiffany lamps
* waking up to the smell of fresh coffee brewing
* Monopoly
* moonlight on the porch
* pretending we don't know Santa is really Dad
* "While Shepherds Watched Their Flocks by Night"
* children in pajamas with feet
* a mountaintop restaurant

Christmas Eve

* the 11:00 p.m. candlelight service
* the anticipation of special moments on Christmas Day
* reading the Christmas story from the Bible together
* caroling on the beach
* arriving home just in time for Christmas
* someone unexpected arriving home just in time for Christmas
* telling "Remember that Christmas when ..." stories with family
* expecting phone calls
* sleeping babies
* snoring dads
* a big round dinner-plate Christmas moon
* surprise guests
* expected guests

But when the time had fully come, God sent his Son, born of a woman, born under law, to redeem those under law, that we might receive the full rights of sons. Because you are sons, God sent the Spirit of his Son into our hearts, the Spirit who calls out, "Abba, Father."

GALATIANS 4:4-6

❋ Mrs. Santa
❋ muffins:
  ❋ poppyseed
  ❋ blueberry
  ❋ apple
  ❋ cinnamon
  ❋ pumpkin
❋ mugs with your name on them
❋ musical figurines:
  ❋ angels
  ❋ the manger scene
  ❋ ice-skaters
  ❋ Santa
  ❋ Christmas trees
❋ a kitten hiding in the nativity stable
❋ my dad reading *The Grinch Who Stole Christmas* to my little brothers
❋ children proudly hanging ornaments they made
❋ vanilla fudge
❋ my fair share of the white meat
❋ quilted homemade picture frames
❋ Santa Claus, Indiana
❋ my hometown Christmas parade
❋ my reflection in an icicle
❋ a kitten pretending to sleep under the tree
❋ a present for my teacher
❋ a present from my teacher

* my favorite city at Christmas:
  * New York
  * Boston
  * Chicago
  * Seattle
  * Tampa
  * Philadelphia
  * Atlanta
  * San Diego
  * Paris
  * Amsterdam
  * London
  * San Juan
* "While You Were Out" notes
* my grandma's "full-to-overflowing-with-relatives" house on Christmas night
* napping on an overstuffed couch
* Nativity figurines made from clothespins with felt costumes
* necklaces with polished stone beads:
  * amber
  * jade
  * turquoise
  * tiger's-eye
  * Petosky stone
* keeping secret craft traditions alive with my grandchildren
* kids trying to stay awake a little longer

* needing two shopping carts at the grocery store
* hand-me-down ski equipment
* golf season pass for Christmas
* the click of grandma's knitting needles
* the chime of the grandfather clock
* kissing on the ski lift
* the UPS man wearing a Santa cap

The idea of the nativity scene began as a way to tell the story of Jesus' birth to those who could neither read it for themselves in the Latin Bible nor understand the language of the Latin masses. The first written record of this tradition tells us that Saint Francis of Assisi organized a living manger scene for his parish in 1223. Then churches everywhere began to encourage the scenes that made the story come alive. Townspeople and parishioners gathered at the manger to sing lovely Christmas hymns. God's love could be better understood through the dramas about the birth of Christ. Nativity displays, whether of large statues or of tiny, carved figurines, made sure everyone could understand this chronicle of God's love.

Mary treasured up all these things and pondered them in her heart.

LUKE 2:19

When mother-love makes all things
    bright,
When joy come with the morning light,
When children gather round their tree,
Thou Christmas Babe, we sing of thee!

TUDOR JENKS

Thanks be to God for his indescribable gift!

2 CORINTHIANS 9:15

I love that you hear songs everywhere—on the radio, in stores, at ski areas; everywhere you go there are free, open expressions about God. No other holiday has so much music and television shows or movies or plays. I savor every minute of this holiday and all the public places where God is worshiped and acknowledged. It is one time of year where I can play meaningful music at work or at home and there seems to be an acceptance and freedom with no condemnation or restriction. Someday God's glory will fill the Earth as the waters cover the Earth, but until that day I am thankful for the celebration of Christmas.

ELISSA KAVOVIT

What I like about Christmas is that you can celebrate it anywhere. I am living in Izmir, Turkey, and I know that no matter what religion a country has adopted, I can still celebrate Christ's birth and the spirit of Christmas cannot be taken away from me.

ASHLEY CRAWFORD

Peanut Butter Scotchies

1 C. Sugar
1 C. Karo
1 C. Peanut Butter
5 C. crisp rice cereal
6 ounces of milk chocolate chips
6 ounces of butterscotch chips

Bring to a boil 1 C. sugar and 1 C. white Karo. Remove from heat as soon as it begins to boil. Stir in 1 C. peanut butter and 5 C. crisp rice cereal. Stir until all cereal is well covered with the mixture. Pat this mixture into a greased 9"x 13" glass baking pan.
To make the topping, melt 6 ounces of chocolate chips and 6 ounces of butterscotch chips in a double boiler.
Pour this over the crisp rice mixture. Let cool, cut and serve. Serves 15 people.

SUBMITTED BY KAREN SMITH

Symbols of Christmas

❈ a white dove, the symbol for the Holy Spirit
❈ the donkey, a symbol of patience
❈ the shepherd, the symbol for Jesus' care and for pastors
❈ Christ is called the Morning Star
❈ gold, the gift of purity, refined by fire

The Christmas tree reminds me of the church, the star on the top of the tree representing Christ, and all of the beautiful ornaments representing the good works of the church members. He is the head of the church and we are the branches.

THOMAS GATELY

A Christmas candle is a lovely thing;
    It makes no noise at all,
But softly gives itself away;
    While quite unselfish, it grows small.

EVA K. LOGUE

JOY TO THE WORLD

Joy to the world, the Lord is come!
Let earth receive her King;
Let every heart prepare Him room,
And heaven and nature sing,
And heaven and nature sing,
And heaven, and heaven, and nature sing.
Joy to the world, the Savior reigns!
Let men their songs employ;
While fields and floods, rocks, hills and plains
Repeat the sounding joy,
Repeat the sounding joy,
Repeat, repeat, the sounding joy.
No more let sins and sorrows grow,
Nor thorns infest the ground;
He comes to make His blessings flow
Far as the curse is found,
Far as the curse is found,
Far as, far as, the curse is found.
He rules the world with truth and grace,
And makes the nations prove
The glories of His righteousness,
And wonders of His love,
And wonders of His love,
And wonders, wonders, of His love.

ISSAC WATTS

❋ a model train racing around the Christmas tree
❋ nut-covered cheese balls
❋ a gigantic pile of coats on the guestroom bed
❋ a grandchild hiding under a gigantic pile of coats on the guestroom bed
❋ oatmeal and raisins for breakfast
❋ office parties
❋ old English carols
❋ a mother's prayer
❋ celebrating a new Christian's first Christmas with them
❋ a gift book about fishing for dad
❋ silk thermals
❋ cotton long johns
❋ Joseph's staff
❋ joy
❋ just strolling downtown, not shopping
❋ kaleidoscopes
❋ a little gift slipped into a Christmas card
❋ a Christmas CD by your favorite recording artist
❋ homemade chicken pot pie
❋ kissing someone special under the mistletoe
❋ a family road trip to Frankenmuth, Michigan
❋ needlework pillowcases
❋ peppermint gum
❋ children running and tumbling in the snow
❋ "Who's got room for dessert?"
❋ Nestle's Quick: chocolate or strawberry

THE SHEPHERDS HAD AN ANGEL

The Shepherds had an angel
The Wise Men had a star,
But what have I, a little child,
To guide me home from far,
Where glad stars sing together,
And singing Angels are?
Christ watches me, His little lamb;
Cares for me day and night,
That I may be His own in heaven
So angels, clad in white,
Shall sing their "Glory, glory"
For my sake in the height.
Lord, I will give my love to Thee,
Than gold much costlier,
Sweeter to Thee than frankincense,
More prized than choicest myrrh;
Lord, make me dearer day by day,
Day by day holier.

CHRISTINA ROSSETTI

* new photos from out-of-town friends
* newborn babies in Santa Claus suits and hats
* ski season passes
* Niagara Falls:
    * the frozen falls with giant icicles lit with red and green spotlights
    * laser light show
    * the frozen mist on the trees and bridges like sugar coating
    * being the only couple in the French restaurant at the top of the spiral tower
* pecan tarts
* no two snowflakes alike
* Norman Rockwell paintings:
    * Santa
    * winter scenes
    * children
    * parents and grandparents
    * the dining table scenes
* not minding that my family is brushing off all that snow on the rug
* a kitten purring as it falls asleep on your lap
* children sitting on Santa's lap
* peanut butter cookies with fork crisscrosses
* nougat

I love Christmas because...

* shopping at Watertower Place in Chicago
* wrapping paper confetti scraps left after you vacuum on Jan. 3
* opening each little door of the Advent calendar
* opening presents with a phone in one hand and someone special on the line
* "You aren't leaving already?"
* orange, lime, and lemon slice candy
* help with the decorations
* doing the decorations all by myself
* oranges covered with whole cloves for an air freshener
* Oreo cookies: original and double-stuffed
* a Nativity scene crocheted in a blanket
* ornaments with names of people who received them
* a backwoods Christmas tree with fishing lures and carved animals
* our family eggnog recipe
* a high school orchestra's Christmas concert
* our prayer circle's Christmas meditation
* our traditional viewing of "It's a Wonderful Life" on Christmas Eve
* a beautiful infant boy in a manger bed
* unwrapping the old-fashioned decorations with Grandma and hearing their history

* outlet malls:
  * Hush Puppy outlet
  * Calvin Klein
  * Lane Bryant
  * sports equipment
  * china
  * kitchen gadget store
  * dollar store
  * discount jewelry
  * athletic shoe store
  * Burlington Coat Factory
  * carpet outlet
  * furniture outlet
  * framing and picture store
* Christmas party at the waterslide in Australia
* homemade Christmas cards on parchment paper
* elementary school craft tables covered in red and green construction paper scraps
* old fashioned button dolls
* little girls learning that their new doll's hair is not going to grow back after they cut it
* the mystery clay gift from your 3rd grader
* "Guess what it is?" "It's a pony!"
* not being able to fit one more thing into the fridge
* Ovaltine
* children trying to wade through the snow, all bundled up in snowsuits

* oyster stuffing
* a big Santa kite on the beach
* packing cookies to send to college students
* painting scenery for the Christmas play
* palm tree Christmas trees

I found the truth of Christmas joy could be found only when the story is completed with Easter. A baby came as a gift to us, but it was not until Easter that the gift was unwrapped and revealed.

It is the beauty of Christmas which points to a victorious Easter and the revelation of the one and only true gift. It is all I need, and in that the joy of Christmas has been restored.

DEANNA COONER

Christmas Day

❊ "I made it myself, Mommy!"

❊ smiles, happy sounds, and a general feeling of joy

❊ watching my family open presents I got them that I know they really wanted

❊ trying on the new clothes

❊ tossing wrapping paper into big trash bags across the room while unwrapping gifts

❊ the Rose Bowl parade

❊ trying out new sleds

❊ opening the most mysterious present first

❊ opening the most mysterious present last

The Light that shines from the humble manger is strong enough to lighten our way to the end of our days.

VITA-RAYS

* pancake syrup:
  * apricot
  * maple
  * peach
  * cherry
  * apple
  * Mrs. Butterworth's
  * Log Cabin
* trees glazed with "sugary" ice
* a 30-ft extension cord that's not being used
* a black horse with silver halter bells
* paper dolls
* Those unforgettable characters from "It's a Wonderful Life":
  * George Bailey
  * Mary
  * Clarence
  * Bert the cop
  * Ernie the cabbie
  * Violet
  * Harry Bailey
  * Uncle Billy
  * Mr. Potter
  * Sam Wainwright
* passing out candles for the Christmas Eve church service

* trying to think up something to say for the home video camera
* patchwork Christmas stockings
* restoring an antique doll to give to your granddaughter for Christmas
* finding a ladybug in the house in December
* coming up with the perfect plan to bake two casseroles, a turkey and the rolls all in the same oven
* peace
* a new puppy for Christmas:
  * smooth short hair
  * fuzzy long hair
  * black or yellow Lab
  * springer spaniel
  * poodle
  * German shepherd
  * Pomeranian
  * Scottie
  * collie
  * Irish setter
  * dachshund
  * West Highland terrier
  * Saint Bernard
  * mystery mixture dog

GOOD CHRISTIAN FRIENDS, REJOICE

Good Christian friends, rejoice
With heart and soul and voice;
Give ye heed to what we say:
Jesus Christ is born today
Good Christian friends, rejoice
With heart and soul and voice;
Now ye hear of endless bliss:
Jesus Christ was born for this
He has opened heaven's door,
And we are blest forevermore,
Christ was born for this!
Christ was born for this.

TRADITIONAL GERMAN CAROL

* that secret pair of gloves that no one can borrow
* having extra gloves for people who forgot theirs
* birdhouses made for your mom in shop class
* peanut brittle
* children's Christmas songs
* pecan Sticky Buns
* people dressed like Dickens characters singing carols at the mall
* people touch more often
* peppermint
* Père Noël
* picking out this year's Christmas cards
* a blue cape with gold stars
* mistletoe hanging from your rear view mirror
* kissing under the mistletoe on your rear view mirror
* a coupon for breakfast in bed drawn in crayon

Christmas in Bethlehem. The ancient dream: a cold, clear night made brilliant by a glorious star, the smell of incense, shepherds and wise men falling to their knees in adoration of the sweet baby, the incarnation of perfect love.

LUCINDA FRANKS

O, HOLY NIGHT

O holy night, the stars are brightly shining;
It is the night of the dear Savior's birth!
Long lay the world in sin and error pining,
Till He appeared and the soul felt its worth.
A thrill of hope, the weary soul rejoices,
For yonder breaks a new and glorious morn.
Fall on your knees, O hear the angel voices!
O night divine, O night when Christ was born!
O night, O holy night, O night divine!
Led by the light of faith serenely beaming,
With glowing hearts by His cradle we stand.
So led by light of a star sweetly gleaming,
Here came the wise men from Orient land.
The King of kings lay thus in lowly manger,
In all our trials born to be our friend!
Truly He taught us to love one another;
His law is love and His Gospel is peace.
Chains shall He break for the slave is our brother
And in His Name all oppression shall cease.
Sweet hymns of joy in grateful chorus raise we,
Let all within us praise His holy Name!

PLACIDE CLAPPEAU

* putting together toys
* decorative tree skirts
* my husband's sloppy attempts of to wrap gifts
* Computer gifts:
  * games
  * a box of new floppy disks
  * a new state-of-the-art mouse
  * mouse pad featuring your favorite art
* sugar plum hand soap
* "All I want for Christmas is my two front teeth."
* The Chipmunks Christmas album
* lost kitties coming home
* trying to name all of Santa's reindeer by memory
* new versions of Christmas carols performed by your favorite musicians
* Christmas concerts held in old theaters
* The smell of a baking Christmas ham
* Christmas-colored socks that jingle when you walk
* snow angels
* having a neighborhood contest to see who can out-decorate each other
* building a fire and roasting marshmallows or popping popcorn
* trying to recite "Twas the Night Before Christmas" from memory

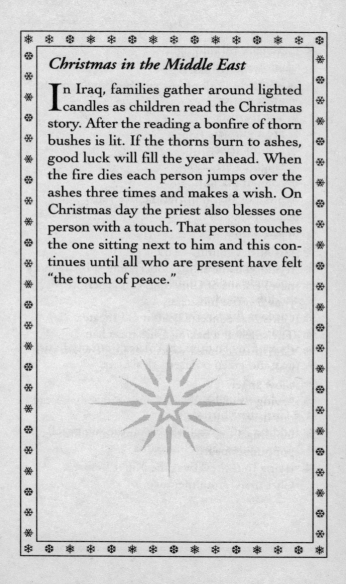

Christmas in the Middle East

In Iraq, families gather around lighted candles as children read the Christmas story. After the reading a bonfire of thorn bushes is lit. If the thorns burn to ashes, good luck will fill the year ahead. When the fire dies each person jumps over the ashes three times and makes a wish. On Christmas day the priest also blesses one person with a touch. That person touches the one sitting next to him and this continues until all who are present have felt "the touch of peace."

❄ Pictionary till midnight:
  ❄ winning at Pictionary
  ❄ losing
  ❄ great artists
  ❄ awful artists
  ❄ great guessers
  ❄ awful guessers
  ❄ laughing art critics
  ❄ colored markers
❄ tree stands that don't let the tree lean
❄ piecrust cookies
❄ pillow shams
❄ piñata
❄ pine bough bunting
❄ pineapple and coconut
❄ childlike wonder
❄ pinecone fireplace starters
❄ a blue-eyed pony
❄ a box of my favorite chocolates from my honey
❄ pink and green poinsettia leaves
❄ pita bread
❄ plaid bunting for the tree
❄ a Christmas birthday
❄ toddlers riding Big Wheels on the sun porch
❄ plastic cups shaped like Santa

* playing detective to try to find out where your presents are hidden before they're wrapped
* poinsettias at the grocery store
* toddlers with pillow wrinkles on their cheeks
* Polaroid camera
* popovers

Your friendship is a glowing ember
Through the year; and each December
From its warm and living spark
We kindle flame against the dark
And with its shining radiance light
Our tree of faith on Christmas night.

THELMA J. LUND

My favorite thing about Christmas is when there is snow falling on Christmas Eve. When the children are finally asleep at the end of all the giggles, last-minute questions, and drinks of water, I turn off all the lights except for those on the Christmas tree. I put the last touches on the presents I've wrapped and pile them under our tree. I look out the window at the dark blue sky and twinkling stars with lacy snowflakes floating to the ground to make a soft white blanket. I am overcome with warmth and peace.

I'll never forget the Christmas that my oldest son almost didn't make it home. He was in the military and was driving home on Christmas Eve from North Carolina to Ohio with some friends when his car was totalled in an accident with a truck. They all rushed to a nearby airport to try and get on a flight standby, but the planes were all full. A taxi driver overheard them and said he would drive them all the way home for the same price as an airline ticket. They all got to our house about three in the morning on Christmas. The best part of Christmas is definitely my family being able to get together.

JANET STEPAK

I HEARD THE BELLS ON CHRISTMAS DAY

I heard the bells on Christmas day
Their old familiar carols play
And mild and sweet the words repeat,
Of peace on earth, good will to men.
I thought how as the day had come,
The belfries of all Christendom
Had roll'd along th' unbroken song
Of peace on earth, good will to men.
And in despair I bow'd my head:
"There is no peace on earth," I said,
"For hate is strong, and mocks the song
Of peace on earth, good will to men."
Then pealed the bells more loud and deep:
"God is not dead, nor doth He sleep;
The wrong shall fail, the right prevail,
With peace on earth, good will to men."
'Til ringing, singing on its way,
The world revolved from night to day,
A voice, a chime, a chant sublime,
Of peace on earth, good will to men!

HENRY WADSWORTH LONGFELLOW

* popping bubblewrap from the packages
* porta-cribs with sleeping infants
* a Christmas Eve dinner for all my friends who do not have family in the area
* posing for family photos in the living room while we wait for dinner
* potpourri
* illuminated stars on top of small-town water towers
* preparing for something special
* pressed-flower bookmarks
* pretending to go to bed so the kids will go
* peanut butter chocolate chip
* puff pastry
* a Christmas Eve sing-along
* pulling the teenagers out of bed on Christmas morning
* toddlers with Christmas bibs
* pull-out sofa beds
* punch with "clouds" of raspberry sherbet in it
* puppies in a box
* a Christmas cookie exchange
* putting gift bows on babies' heads
* quiche: four cheese, spinach, bacon, veggie
* quilted Bible covers
* radio-controlled cars: racers, monster trucks, Barbie's pink convertible
* rainbows reflected on the wall from icicles
* raspberry fizzy punch

Christmas in the City

* a yellow cab ride
* street vendors
* wondering who is in that big limo
* being the one riding in the big limo
* "Walk" and "Don't Walk" lights
* a warm bus ride
* newsstands
* the coffee shop:
  * café au lait
  * cappuccino
  * latte
  * mocha java
  * frappuccino
  * Starbucks' flavor of the day
  * ten varieties of pastry
  * six different muffins
  * black coffee from Dunkin' Donuts
  * fifty varieties of donuts
* the old clock downtown
* little old ladies carrying their dogs
* Chinese dinners:
  * egg rolls
  * hot and sour soup
  * egg-drop soup
  * cashew chicken
  * sweet and sour chicken
  * fried rice
  * fortune cookies
  * white paper cartons with wire handles

* reading in a big comfy chair:
  * *A Pilgrim at Tinker's Creek*
  * *Little Women*
  * *On the Banks of Plum Creek*
  * The Gospel of Luke
* icicles bending evergreen branches
* ready and willing volunteers
* toddlers playing with the gift wrap instead of the gift
* real candles on the tree
* red and green balloons on the mailbox for a Christmas party
* any kind of candy that comes from my Christmas stocking
* any kind of candy that I swiped from my brother's Christmas stocking
* red and silver barrettes for little girls
* reflecting on what the birth of our Savior means to me
* chocolate coins in net bags
* reindeer with sleigh bells
* relationships restored
* how Grandma gives us credit for any little help with Christmas dinner
* reliving Christmas through our children
* remembering that certain moment in time— the birth of Christ
* revolving gel lights changing colors on a tree
* Rhode Island Red rooster alarm

After sixty-eight years, I have many wonderful Christmas memories. One was when I was seventeen, and my friends and I went caroling in our little town in southern Ohio on Christmas Eve. It was so warm that year, we took off our coats. The moon was huge and bright, and it started snowing—large, beautiful flakes that fell in our hair and on our clothes. It was unbelievable on such a warm night when everything was so quiet except for our carols.

I also cherish the memories of my four children and how excited they were about Christmas. How they would peek around the corner of the stairway, trying to look for Santa. Meanwhile their father, hidden away in another room, put the last bolts in a wagon or bike. These are just a few of my wonderful visions of Christmases past. I thank God for all this—without him and his Son, it would not have happened. Thank you, Lord!

CONSTANCE THOMPSON

The Christmas after my stepfather passed away, my mom felt she couldn't bear to get out all the decorations they had hung together for so many years. I helped her buy all new decorations and make a "lady's Christmas tree" with pink and gold accents on a white artificial tree. She put her china doll collection around the tree and invited all her girlfriends over to admire it.

PAT MATUSZAK

* rhubarb, cherry, peach, apple or chocolate cobbler
* ribbon candy
* hot cross buns
* chocolate croissants
* Rice Crispy treats with:
  * chocolate icing
  * red and green sprinkles
  * chocolate chips
* riding a float in the Christmas parade
* road maps spread out all over the table as we plan a trip
* roasted chestnuts
* holiday care packages for kids in the military:
  * dozens of cookies
  * cough drops
  * stamps
  * writing paper and cards

❆ red and green socks
❆ granola power bars
❆ powdered soup and coffee packets
❆ packets of nuts
❆ candy bars
❆ how everyone at Grandfather's church knows
his name
❆ Rockford, Michigan shopping village
❆ rocking horse ornaments:
  ❆ wooden
  ❆ tin
  ❆ plastic
  ❆ rocking reindeer
❆ rolling pins:
  ❆ marble
  ❆ wooden
  ❆ plastic
  ❆ decorated with a Christmas design
❆ rootbeer barrel candy
❆ rose hip tea
❆ chocolate-covered cherries
❆ toddlers falling asleep at the table
❆ rows of coat hooks in the hallway, all filled with
coats
❆ Rudolph
❆ Dancer
❆ Prancer
❆ Comet
❆ Cupid

* ❄ Vixen
* ❄ Donner
* ❄ Blitzen
* ❄ Russian nesting dolls
* ❄ s'mores
* ❄ sage
* ❄ sailboats with Christmas lights and decorations
* ❄ salespeople who say, "Merry Christmas!"
* ❄ salted sunflower seeds
* ❄ Salvation Army bands singing carols

O God, who makes us glad with the yearly remembrance of the birth of your only Son Jesus Christ; Grant that as we joyfully receive him for our Redeemer, so we may with sure confidence behold him when he comes ... who lives and reigns with you and the Holy Spirit, one God, world without end. Amen.

CHRISTMAS DAY PRAYER
FROM *THE BOOK OF COMMON PRAYER*

Christmas Traditions Around the World

In Greece, 40 days of fasting precede a Christmas feast, which always features "christopsomo" or Christ Bread. These large, sweet loaves are shaped and engraved with images that reflect the family's profession.

To remember the star of Bethlehem, in Poland, the Christmas meal does not begin until the first star appears in the sky. The feast is made up of 12 courses, one for each apostle and an extra chair is set at the table for a stranger, or the Holy Spirit to share the meal.

In Venezuela, worshipers often roller skate through the streets to attend the Mis de Auginaldo or early morning mass which is held from Dec. 16 through 24.

The joy of the shepherds is remembered in Ethiopia, where a game called Ganna is played with hooked staffs on Jan 7 by many of the men and boys.

* how my mother always laments the ripping apart of beautifully wrapped gifts
* how my brother and dad always throw wadded up bunches of paper around the room after opening gifts
* how my cats play with the Christmas ornaments on the tree
* the magical look that mall takes on
* tall, thick advent candles
* tape
* scissors
* ribbons
* bows
* gold, red, and pine-green wrapping paper
* Christmas cactuses in bloom
* huge trays with every kind of yummy treat piled on top
* last-minute shopping
* boughs of fresh cut evergreens dusted with snow
* china with holly painted on
* an excited child-like expression on the face of an adult
* electronic greeting cards that play jingle bells
* poinsettias in red, white, and pink
* popcorn strings
* unwinding garland
* how my mother tapes every one of her Christmas cards to the wall

Christmas, my child, is love in action ... When you love someone, you give to them, as God gives to us. The greatest gift He ever gave was the Person of His Son, sent to us in human form so that we might know what God the Father is really like! Every time we love, every time we give, it's Christmas.

DALE EVANS ROGERS

I used to like white Christmases, until I moved to Florida. Now I like green Christmases! I enjoy the palm trees and sand, like my Savior must have in Jerusalem.

But one of my favorite things is finding out what my son wants the most (which is not what he necessarily asks for) and telling him that it's a present from Jesus because the Lord knew what was in his heart.

There's no Santa conflict, because when he was only two years old he came to the conclusion (on his own) that Santa was one of Jesus' angels. When another preschooler challenged him with why Santa eats the goodies if Jesus gives them, he quickly responded, 'Cause Jesus shares.' All I can say is, "out of the mouths of babes."

* satin sheets
* hot chocolate with whipped cream
* sausage stuffing
* Internet shopping
* saying grace before dinner
* Scottie dogs in little plaid capes
* seashell wreaths:
  * tiger shells
  * butterfly wings
  * conches
  * coquinas
  * curls
  * cat's-paws
  * olives
  * angel wings
  * clamshells
  * whelks
  * murexes
  * scallops
  * Chinese hats
  * coral
  * sea horses
  * sea stars
  * sand dollars

* Sanka
* toaster pastry
* Santa arriving on a fire truck
* toddlers carefully holding those delicate ornaments
* scent of Pine Sol from the clean kitchen
* school canceled because of snow
* secrets and surprises for everyone
* instant cappuccino mix
* serving Christmas dinner at a homeless shelter
* setting the Christmas table together
* chocolate-covered coconut candy
* illuminated wire figures:
  * Santa and reindeer
  * angels
  * nativity
  * stars
  * miniature churches
* sewing costumes for Christmas angels
* the Hallmark store
* the hats from chocolate Santas
* "God bless us every one!"
* the high school marching band in the Christmas parade
* "four calling birds"

THE FIRST NOEL

The first Noel the angel did say
Was to certain poor shepherds in fields as they lay;
In fields where they lay tending their sheep,
On a cold winter's night that was so deep.
Noel, Noel, Noel, Noel,
Born is the King of Israel.
They looked up and saw a star
Shining in the east, beyond them far;
And to the earth it gave great light,
And so it continued both day and night.
Noel, Noel, Noel, Noel,
Born is the King of Israel.
And by the light of that same star
Three Wise Men came from country far;
To seek for a King was their intent,
And to follow the star wherever it went.
Noel, Noel, Noel, Noel,
Born is the King of Israel.
Then entered in those Wise Men three,
Full reverently upon the knee,
And offered there, in His presence,
Their gold and myrrh and frankincense.
Noel, Noel, Noel, Noel,
Born is the King of Israel.

OLD ENGLISH CAROL

Early on Christmas Morning, when it is still very dark, I sit on the fireplace hearth in my parents' bedroom. The fire crackles at my back, and they sit up in bed drinking coffee. We are all quiet as we watch the snow drift down upon our sleepy little street outside. There are no bustling cars, no loud voices—just my parents, me, and Jesus-reminding us of why we celebrate his birth. For this thirty-year-old "kid," that is heaven.

I like Christmas because it gives me a chance to remember. Some people buy T-shirts or knickknacks when they are on trips. We collect Christmas ornaments. As a missionary family, we travel a lot, and our Christmas ornament collection anchors us as a family from move to move, especially as we are going on Christmas number six away from our home country. And when no "ornament" is available, we make our own. In our collection we have a tiny bale of cotton — a remembrance of the oldest hardware store in Huntsville, Alabama. We have a carved wooden elephant from Chiang Mai, Thailand, with memories of conferences there; a silver jeepney taken from a key chain in the Philippines purchased during seminary studies. Each ornament is an important link to show us where we have been, where God has brought us, and how life with him brings us further adventures yet to be seen on our tree.

❊ sharing
❊ shepherd boys
❊ Shetland ponies giving rides
❊ the wise men's traveling tents
❊ shiny Christmas banners
❊ Shipshewana's flea market
❊ shopping at the Christmas village
❊ chocolate-covered sea foam candy
❊ shopping together at the mall and hiding what
  we bought for each other
❊ show horses in black harnesses
❊ homemade taffy
❊ showing children the Christmas book you
  loved when you were their age
❊ shrimp cocktail
❊ silk pj's
❊ silly games at parties:
  ❊ orange-pass relay
  ❊ spoon-drop relay
  ❊ story games
  ❊ trivia contests
  ❊ the memory game
  ❊ straw in the bottle
  ❊ what's in your purse?
❊ the whole world stands still to celebrate the
  advent of One life

* silver and gold bunting for the tree
* singing "Happy Birthday" to Jesus
* homemade milk carton candles
* sitting in bed drinking coffee early on Christmas morning
* sitting together in the evenings by the glow of the Christmas lights in the house
* Christmas clothes are more furry, fuzzy, and fun
* skiers:
  * little kids learning
  * grown-ups learning
  * mighty mites speeding
  * a smooth run
  * a graceful fall
  * a "yard sale" fall
* sledding at a favorite hill
* sleeping over at friends' houses
* chocolates wrapped in red and green foil
* slush splashing
* smiling, happy faces all around
* the whole family going to a candlelight church service together
* homemade fudge with pecans
* smoked salmon
* sneaking down to see the tree just before dawn on Christmas morning

* snitching raw cookie dough
* snow drifting down outside just before day-break on Christmas morning
* snowshoe prints
* snuggling together in a big fluffy quilt
* the white rose and the poinsettia symbolize the Nativity
* socks with toes in them
* someone nice warming up the car for you

O God, help us to remember that the dear Lord Jesus came to earth and lived among us. He is indeed Emmanuel, "God with us." If you are with us we need not fear, for you are greater than all that might come against us. Fill our hearts with great confidence and hope. For the Redeemer's sake. Amen.

DON SANFORD

Date Pudding

1 C. chopped dates	1/2 C. white sugar
1 C. flour	1 C. chopped walnuts
1 Tsp. vanilla	2 C. boiling water
1 T. butter	1 C. brown sugar
1 Tsp. baking powder	1 T. shortening
1/4 Tsp. salt	1/2 C. milk
Whipped topping	

Mix in a 9"x13" glass baking dish: 2 C. boiling water, 1 T. butter, and 1 C. brown sugar. Keep this mixture hot while mixing the batter.

In another bowl mix together:1/2 C. sugar, 1 tsp. baking powder, 1 T. shortening, 1/4 tsp. salt, 1/2 C. milk, 1 C. chopped dates, 1 C. flour, 1 C. chopped walnuts, and 1 tsp. vanilla.

Drop this mixture by spoonfuls into the hot water, butter and brown sugar mixture.

Bake in a 350 degree oven for 30-35 minutes. When cooled, top with whipped topping

SUBMITTED BY KAREN SMITH

The message of Christmas is that the visible material world is bound to the invisible spiritual world.

ANONYMOUS

Many merry Christmases, friendships, great accumulation of cheerful recollections, affection on earth, and Heaven at last for all of us.

CHARLES DICKENS

Instead of being a time of unusual behavior Christmas is perhaps the only time in the year when people can obey their natural impulses and express their true sentiments without feeling self-conscious and, perhaps, foolish. Christmas in short, is about the only chance a man has to be himself.

FRANCIS C. FARLEY

* Christmas cookie jars:
  * jolly Santa
  * bears
  * dolls
  * gingerbread houses
* sopping socks drying by the fireplace
* sparkly expressions on children's faces when they whisper a secret to Santa
* spearmint-leaf jelly mints
* special Christmas shows at the planetarium
* speeding on snowmobiles
* knit toboggan hats
* crochet mittens
* wool gloves
* white parkas
* alpine-trim coats
* goofy ski hats
* spiced almonds
* spilling the Styrofoam "macaroni" when we open packages.
* the sun shines more brightly on the snow at Christmas
* spiral staircase banisters draped in greenery and red ribbons
* spray-painted tree branches from pines, oaks, maples, and holly in gold, red or silver

* stained-glass angels on lampposts
* star candleholders
* Christmas cookie ornaments
* Star Trek Christmas tree ornaments
  * The Enterprise
  * Mr. Spock
  * Captain Kirk
  * Scotty
* starlight through a skylight
* homemade Dutch almond sticks
* starting a popcorn-throwing fight
* stationery with your initials on it
* staying home with just the two of us
* steam curling up from cocoa
* stick-on name and address labels
* sticky notes everywhere
* the icy green December sky at the horizon:
  * pink and blue above
  * half-moon at the zenith
* ice carvings
* winter carnivals
* a box of mixed chocolates to share with your sister who only likes cream centers when you only like caramels
* an anniversary diamond ring in your stocking
* marks made on the wall showing how much the children have grown each year

Twas the night before Christmas; in one room of the house
Some creatures were stirring (too much noise, not a mouse!).
Our boys in their room, supposedly sleeping,
Were doing a lot of talking and peeping
And dreaming of Star Wars and barbells and drums
And footballs and paint sets and so on and on.
I was a bit curious as I heard all their chatter
And wondered just what in the world was the matter.
I listened a minute, then reprovingly said,
"Is that all Christmas means—just what you will get?"
"Well, Mother, we realize it's Jesus' birthday,
But how can we give Him a gift Christmas Day?

He made everything that there is on this earth,

So what could we give Him that's of any worth?"

I thought of an answer already provided

And replied to their question in tones quite decided:

"If you give some cold water to someone who needs it,

You're giving to Jesus. Let's turn to Matthew and read it."

Soon two little boys were asleep in their beds,

But thoughts were still going around in my head....

That verse was so easy—too easy—to say,

But how many needs had I noticed that day?

Inasmuch as ye have done it unto one of the least of these my brethren, you have done it unto Me.

MATTHEW 25:40 KJV

JOY JACOBS

* finding extra candy in January that you forgot to put in the stockings
* your bell-bottom jeans came back in style and you get to hand them down to your daughter for a surprise Christmas present
* your bell-bottom jeans came back in style and you can give them to yourself as a Christmas present because you can actually still get into them!
* getting to the post office with your Christmas packages just before the lunch rush
* a Christmas variety show at Bearcreek Farms

Christmas is the day that holds time together.

ALEXANDER SMITH

* peanut butter cookies baking
* stirring your coffee with a candy cane
* stomping your feet on the doormat
* the sound of popping popcorn
* stopping to hear the praises to God in carols
* stories about old-fashioned Christmases
* streudel:
  * raspberry
  * cherry
  * cream cheese
  * blueberry
  * apple
* Christmas Day football games in the yard
* stringing popcorn
* striped candy canes on the tree
* getting to the post office before it closes
* seeing people actually smile as they wait in line
  to mail boxes at the post office
* puppy pretending to growl and be fierce
* strolling through the neighborhood and waving
  to friends
* sugar eyes from chocolate reindeer
* sunflower nut bread
* surprise phone calls
* swirled rye bread
* the sound of people coming to open the door
* taffy Christmas tree mints

I sometimes think we expect too much of Christmas Day. We try to crowd into it the long arrears of kindliness and humanity of the whole year. As for me, I like to take my Christmas a little at a time, all through the year. And thus I drift along into the holidays—let them overtake me unexpectedly—waking up some fine morning and suddenly saying to myself: "Why this is Christmas Day!

DAVID GRAYSON

Love came down at Christmas;
Love all lovely, love divine;
Love was born at Christmas,
Stars and angels gave the sign.

CHRISTINA ROSSETTI

* stuffed soft-sculpture ornaments:
  * Santa and Mrs. Claus
  * fruit baskets
  * apples
  * grapes
  * bananas
  * hearts with lace
* Swanson's mini pot pies
* Christmas dishes
* Swedish "star carriers"
* sweet potato pie and whipped cream
* taking time with one special person
* tapestry throws
* tartines with glazed pear topping
* tassled bouclé throw blankets
* teaching a child how to string popcorn
* tealights
* teardrop crystal ornaments
* sugarplum fairy ballerinas
* teddy bears dressed in red sweaters
* telling a Christmas secret into a child's tiny ear
* the sound of doves in the stable rafters
* terry cloth robes
* that big old dining room table we crowded around at our grandparents' house

❊ that certain feeling of love that Christmastime inspires

❊ that green Jell-O creation

❊ that guy on your block who goes way over-board with the Christmas lights and invites you to help take them down every spring

❊ the hope to keep Christmas in our hearts all year

❊ that jingling noise when the kitten tries to climb the Christmas tree

❊ that serious look of concentration on faces as they try to remember words to carols

❊ that sleepy rocking chair creak

❊ the angel ornament's face glowing from the lights on the tree

❊ Christmas golf balls:
  ❊ red and green
  ❊ candy cane striped
  ❊ "Merry Christmas"
  ❊ with Santa on them

❊ the antique card my Grandmother sends each year from her collection

❊ the aroma of turkey and ham both cooking at once

❊ the artificial Christmas tree aisle at Sears

❊ the baaing of lambs

* the bakery:
  * bakers in white aprons
  * angel food cake
  * scones
  * chocolate bread
  * half-price shelf
  * layer cakes with icing decoration
  * mini cakes in boxes
  * carrot cake with carrot-shaped decorations
  * a baker's dozen
* the bare feet of shepherd boys
* puppy learning to do a real bark
* big piles of wrapping paper after all the gifts are opened
* a big red bow on our front-door Christmas wreath
* birds at our Christmas feeder:
  * house wrens
  * tufted titmice
  * sparrows
  * junco
  * blue jays
* the blessings Jesus gave all of us
* Christmas guest towels
* the Bright and Morning Star
* a lost puppy coming home

The time draws near the birth of Christ.
  The moon is hid, the night is still;
  The Christmas bells from hill to hill
  Answer each other in the mist.
Four voices of four hamlets round,
  From far and near, on mead and moor,
  Swell out and fail, as if a door
  Were shut between me and the sound;
Each voice four changes on the wind,
  That now dilate, and now decrease,
  Peace and goodwill, goodwill and
  peace,
  Peace and goodwill, to all mankind.
But they my troubled spirit rule,
  For they controll'd me when a boy;
  They bring me sorrow touch'd with
  joy,
  The merry, merry bells of Yule.

Our voices took a higher range;
  Once more we sang: "They do not die
  Nor lose their mortal sympathy,
  Nor change to us, although they
  change;
"Rapt from the fickle and the frail
  With gather'd power, yet the same,
  Pierces the keen seraphic flame
  From orb to orb, from veil to veil."
Rise, happy morn, rise, holy morn,
  Draw forth the cheerful day from
  night:
O Father, touch the east, and light
  The light that shone when Hope was
  born.

ALFRED, LORD TENNYSON

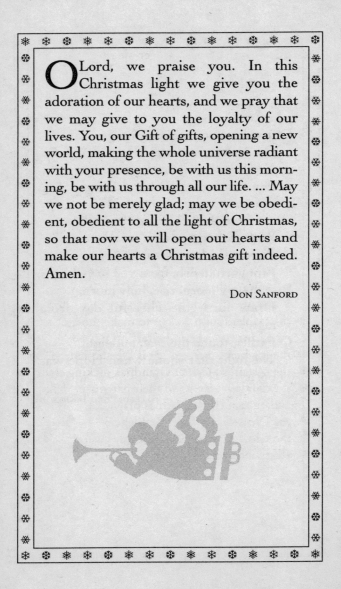

OLord, we praise you. In this Christmas light we give you the adoration of our hearts, and we pray that we may give to you the loyalty of our lives. You, our Gift of gifts, opening a new world, making the whole universe radiant with your presence, be with us this morning, be with us through all our life. ... May we not be merely glad; may we be obedient, obedient to all the light of Christmas, so that now we will open our hearts and make our hearts a Christmas gift indeed. Amen.

DON SANFORD

❄ punch with a frozen ginger-ale ring
❄ the candy store:
  ❄ a skinny shopkeeper
  ❄ a chubby shopkeeper
  ❄ candy toys
  ❄ strings of rock candy
  ❄ swizzle sticks
  ❄ candy apples
  ❄ chocolate apples
  ❄ chocolate roses
  ❄ Gummy Worms
  ❄ chocolate racecars
  ❄ gourmet jelly beans
  ❄ saltwater taffy
  ❄ ten varieties of fudge
  ❄ the weekly candy special
❄ the caroler that manages to make those of us who can't sing sound better
❄ the celebration of all that is life and redeeming
❄ the certain squeak of Grandpa's rocking chair
❄ the children waving to their parents in the audience at the Christmas play
❄ the Christmas bells in Bethlehem
❄ the Christmas sermon from my pastor
❄ Christmas ivy place mats

❄ the creamy color of eggnog
❄ crisp air
❄ the dinner bell
❄ an evergreen Christmas tree, a symbol of eternal life and God's eternal love
❄ an illuminated star on top of the Christmas tree
❄ the fire station with a big Christmas wreath
❄ the bookstore:
  ❄ the gift book section
  ❄ the calendar aisle
  ❄ the children's corner
  ❄ the poetry section
  ❄ the travel aisle
  ❄ the photo book section
  ❄ the humor section
  ❄ soothing music in the background
❄ the clicking of puppy paws on linoleum
❄ the colors red and green get disassociated with merely "stop" and "go" and get to be real colors for a little while

God's gifts put man's best dreams to shame.

ELIZABETH BARRETT BROWNING

* the fireplace mantel:
  * pictures of family
  * decorations toddlers can't reach
  * candles
* the first frost
* the five-pointed star, a symbol of God's revelation
* the frilly day bed in Grandma's guest room
* the smell of wood smoke in the air:
  * applewood,
  * hickory
  * pine branches
  * charcoal fires
* angel footsteps in straw
* The Game of Life
* the gift wrap counter
* gold stands for glory
* Christmas laughter and conversation coming up through the big furnace vents to the bedroom
* the glitter of the season
* the glory of angel choirs
* the glow you feel on Christmas Eve
* the golden capes of the magi
* the good silver
* the Grinch
* the Hallelujah chorus

Wishing a "Merry Christmas" Around the World

Arabic	Milad Majid
Argentine	Feliz Navidad
Bulgarian	Tchestita Koleda
Cambodian	Soursdey Noel
Mandarin Chinese	Sheng Dankuai Le
Croatian	Sretan Bozic
Danish	Glædelig Jul
Dutch	Vrolijk Kerstfeest
Filipino	Maligayang Pasko
Finnish	Hauskaa Joulua
French	Joyeux Noël
Gaelic	Nollaig Shona Dhuit
German	Froehliche Weihnachten
Greek	Kala Christouyenna
Hawaiian	Mele Kalikimaka
Hebrew	Mo'adim Lesimkha. Chena tova
Hungarian	Kellemes Karacsonyi unnepeket
Indonesian	Selamat Hari Natal
Iraqi	Idah Saidan Wa Sanah Jadidah
Italian	Buon Natale
Japanese	Meri Kurisumasu
Korean	Sung Tan Jul Chuk Ha
Navajo	Merry Kashmis
Norwegian	Gledelig Jul

Pennsylvania Dutch	En frehlicher Grischtdaag
Polish	Wesolych Swiat Bozego Narodzenia
Portuguese	Feliz Natal
Rumanian	Sarbatori Fericite
Russian	S Rozhdestvom Kristovym
Serbian	Hristos se rodi
Slovakian	Sretan Bozic
Samoan	Manuea le Karisimasi
Scots Gaelic	Nollaig chridheil huibh
Slovak	Vesele Vianoce. A stastlivy Novy
Spanish	Feliz Navidad
Swedish	God Jul
Tahitian	Ia ora'na no te noere
Thai	Suksan Christmas
Turkish	Noeliniz Ve Yeni Yiliniz Kutlu
Ukrainian	Z Rizdvom Krystovym
Vietnamese	Chuc Mung Giang Sinh
Welsh	Nadolig Llawen

Christmas is a wonderful time for looking for the best in others. If someone in your life has been a blessing to you, why not tell that person, "I see an angel in you and your good work"? A warm thank you or card of appreciation can light someone else's day. Don't forget to thank children for the little things they do. They will remember and learn by your example to show appreciation.

To make a special thank you for angels who've blessed your life, cut out a small pair of wings from lace, felt, leftover Christmas cards, or construction paper. Glue a small jingle bell onto the front and write "Thank you" on the back. You can string a piece of gold or silver trim ribbon through the top to make a hanger for it, or you can pin it to your "angel's" clothing.

PAT MATUSZAK

Joseph also went up from the town of Nazareth in Galilee to Judea, to Bethlehem the town of David, because he belonged to the house and line of David. He went there to register with Mary, who was pledged to be married to him and was expecting a child. While they were there, the time came for the baby to be born, and she gave birth to her firstborn, a son. She wrapped him in cloths and placed him in a manger, because there was no room for them in the inn.

And there were shepherds living out in the fields nearby, keeping watch over their flocks at night. An angel of the Lord appeared to them, and the glory of the Lord shone around them, and they were terrified. But the angel said to them, "Do not be afraid. I bring you good news of great joy that will be for all the people. Today in the town of David a Savior has been born to you; he is Christ the Lord. This will be a sign to you: You will find a baby wrapped in cloths and lying in a manger."

LUKE 2:4-12

* the Hope of all the world was born
* the humility of Jesus' manger bed; he became poor that all could become rich
* the hush of angel wings
* the illuminated Nativity scene in front of the church
* the jingle bell on a boutique's front door
* Christmas lights in a flowerpot lamp
* the kids' table
* the laugh lines around my Granddad's smile
* the library:
    * Christmas story time
    * the children's section,
    * a comfortable chair in a corner
    * that nice librarian saying, "Shhhhhh" with a smile on her face
* angel pins:
    * crocheted
    * gold
    * silver
    * linen
    * crystal
    * pewter
    * wooden
    * porcelain
* the light of a few flickering candles on the dining table

Christmas—that magic blanket that wraps itself about us, that something so intangible that it is like a fragrance. It may weave a spell of nostalgia. Christmas may be a day of feasting, or of prayer, but always it will be a day of remembrance—a day in which we think of everything we have ever loved.

AUGUSTA E. RUNDELL

May no gift be too small to give, nor too simple to receive, which is wrapped in thoughtfulness, and tied with love.

L. O. BAIRD

THE FRIENDLY BEASTS

Jesus our Brother, kind and good,
Was humbly born in a stable rude.
And the friendly beasts around Him stood;
Jesus our Brother, kind and good.

"I," said the donkey, shaggy and brown,
"I carried His mother up hill and down;
I carried His mother to Bethlehem town.
"I," said the donkey, shaggy and brown.

"I," said the cow, all white and red,
"I gave Him my manger for His bed;
I gave Him my hay to pillow His head."
"I," said the cow, all white and red.

"I," said the sheep with the curly horn,
"I gave Him wool for His blanket warm;
He wore my coat on Christmas morn."
"I," said the sheep, with the curly horn.

"I," said the dove from the rafters high,
"I cooed Him to sleep that He should not cry;
We cooed Him to sleep, my mate and I."

"I," said the dove from the rafters high.
"I," said the camel, yellow and black,
"Over the desert, upon by back
I brought Him a gift in the Wise Men's pack,"
"I," said the camel, yellow and black.
Thus every beast by some good spell,
In the stable dark was glad to tell
Of the gift he gave Emmanuel,
The gift he gave Emmanuel.

FRENCH FOLK CAROL

* "glory to God in the highest"
* the little drummer boy
* The Littlest Angel
* the lodge snack shop:
    * soup-bowl-size mugs of hot chocolate
    * chicken soup
    * varieties of pizza
    * macaroni and cheese
    * tomato soup
    * nachos and cheese
* "Merry Christmas to all, and to all a good night!"
* the love of Christ we see in each other
* the Magi's escape from Herod
* the many different versions of "O Holy Night"
* the maple sugar candy Grandma always shares

Christmas in Italy

It Italy, the main exchange of gift doesn't occur until January 6th, the day traditionally believed that the Wise Men reached the baby Jesus. Italy has La Befana who brings gifts for the good and punishment for the bad. She is the same character as Russia's Babouschka who refused to give the Wise Men food and shelter.

Banana Split Cake

2 C. Graham cracker crumbs
2 C. sugar
1 stick butter melted
1 Large can of crushed pineapple
2-3 Large bananas

Use the back of a spoon to press the Graham cracker crumbs into the bottom of a 9" x 13" glass baking dish. This will form the dessert's crust. Bake the crust 5 minutes at 350 degrees. Let it cool.

Mix together 2 8-ounce packages of cream cheese, 2 cups of sugar, 1 tsp. vanilla and pour over the cooled crust. Slice 2 or 3 large bananas and place over the mixture.

Drain the crushed pineapple and spread it over the cream cheese mixture. Top with whipped topping. Serve immediately. Serves 10-15 people.

SUBMITTED BY KAREN SMITH

Grandma Fran Remembers Christmas

When I was a little girl living in upstate New York with my mother, father and sister, we had very specific things that were always observed at Christmas.

The tree was never put up and decorated until Christmas Eve. During the week before Christmas we would go to get the tree. It was always a 6-foot-tall Balsam. Sometimes, when it was snowy, we would walk to the nearby tree lot, pulling a sled to carry home our prize. It was always cold and most of the time there was fresh white snow frosting everything. It was so beautiful and festive. We would walk along with a happy step singing Christmas Carols just for our own enjoyment.

Trimming the tree was a special family event. We had snacks and shared putting the lights, ornaments and tinsel on our gorgeous tree. It was such fun. After the festivities it was bedtime, at least for me. The rest of the family had special projects to finish before the big day. I can remember sneaking out of bed one year and peeking down the stairs to watch my Dad and Sister set up my new dollhouse. I hardly slept a wink for the rest of the night.

Christmas Day we were up at 5:00 or 6:00 a.m. I could no longer stand the wait. Let's get on with this!

Gifts were opened and shared with high excitement. They were always well worth the wait. Later that day we celebrated with dinner. What a grand time of sharing a delicious meal, playing new games, and trying out any new skis, sleds or skates in the snow.

When I became the mother of three precocious boys Christmas changed a good bit. We still put up the tree on Christmas Eve. However, depending on where we were living, sometimes there was no snow. We secured the tree at a lot and brought it home in the trunk of the car. We still bought a Balsam.

Our boys were always eager to see what was in the brightly wrapped packages and could hardly wait until Christmas morning. So we allowed them to open one gift on Christmas Eve. What a huge decision it was for them! How do you choose just the right package? They managed, however after much consideration. Some family fun time followed and then they were tucked in for the night with a stern warning NOT to get out of bed.

Now those energetic boys have children of their own and I am a Grandma. I now live in the warm South so we have made more changes to our Christmas traditions. We rarely see snow, here in Louisiana, but when there is enough for snowmen, each yard has its own creation, like as snowman invasion!

In this part of the South, Christmas trees and decorations go up December 1 or earlier. Now that is just too soon for me! I did agree to putting it up the Sunday before Christmas but no sooner.

The ornaments for our tree include old ones from my childhood and a big collection that were handmade by friends. I call them my friendship ornaments. As we put them on the tree it is like looking through an album of all my friends. As each one is tenderly placed on the tree it brings fond memories of that person.

One of our families most cherished traditions, is actually begun on Thanksgiving Day. We take a group picture of the entire family. The picture is then made in to calendars and sent as a Christmas present to each one. There have been only two occasions that anyone was missing from this picture in eleven years. That is until last year.

Our granddaughter was married in October and moved to Michigan. Due to the distance, they were not able to be with us on Thanksgiving. We compensated, however by putting their wedding picture in a prominent place in the photo. So in a sense we were all together.

So with this marriage, it starts again, a new family and a new home in a new state. Old traditions will remain and new ones will be found and added.

May all your traditions bring you joy and happiness . . . especially the greatest tradition of all—praising God for sending us his Son!

FRANCES KOGLER

* the movie "Holiday Inn"
* Christmas music in the stores
* angel wings
* the music store:
    * jazz CDs
    * Christmas albums
    * comedy favorites
    * kids' albums
    * top forty hits
* a Nativity scene by candlelight
* the neighborhood block party on Christmas Eve
* the nice lady who directs the Christmas play
* the northern lights
* the Ohio Hartville Kitchen's Amish cooking
* the old ceramic tile fireplace at my grandparents' home
* the old family Bible
* opportunities to tell about Christ
* the Opryland Hotel decorated for Christmas
* Christmas parades
* peace from God that transcends all races
* the quiet chime of a mantel clock
* traditional English carols
* the reflection in glass balls hanging on the Christmas tree
* Salvation Army kettles
* the scent of pine needles when you run the vacuum cleaner on January 24th

* the Scouts marching in the parade
* the secret miracle in a tiny village
* Christmas photo postcards
* the seven archangels
* wise old bearded shepherds
* the shepherds' lambs
* the silhouette of three kings on a hill
* angels as God's messengers
* the silverware chest
* the singers at Disney World wearing Victorian caroling costumes in 80° weather
* fruitcake
* the ski hill:
    * the view from the top
    * the view from the bottom
    * tow-ropes, gondolas
    * lift chairs
    * bunny hill
    * black diamond
    * the back country run
    * cross-country trails
* the sleeping hamlets of ancient Israel
* Christmas pillow shams
* wise men still seek Jesus
* the smell and sound of slicing apples
* the sound of church bells
* fuzzy pink slippers
* the magical transformation that stores go through during the night of October 31

When Jesus Smiled

The cattle lay still in darkened stalls;
    The smell of the hay was sweet;
Joseph kept watch through the long, still night
    At Mary's feet.
The windows were black and barred in the inn;
    The flocks on the hills were asleep;
Mary did look on the Babe by her side,
    And her thoughts were deep.
Timidly up to the manger crept two
    Young children, seeking to find
Shelter and rest. One boy was deaf;
    The other blind.
The face of Mary was tender and calm
    As Joseph made room for them.
Nearer they came, till they knelt in the straw
    At her garment's hem.

Softly she crooned a lullaby low,
    And a great star lilied the night.
The singing was sweet to the one little waif
    To the other, the light.
Close to the heart of His mother lay,
    Like a blossom, the lovely Christ Child.
Softly He stirred and opened His eyes
    And slowly He smiled.
Suddenly then a wonderful thing,
    A beautiful thing, occurred:
The little blind boy cried, "Look, oh, look!"
    And the deaf boy heard.

MARY J. ELMENDORF

* gathering the family around the piano
* the sun shines more brightly on the sand at Christmas
* the surprise on neighbors' faces when they open the door to our caroling group
* the tapping of a dog's wagging tail
* Christmas posters made by Sunday school classes
* playing Christmas tunes during the whole month of December
* beginning to play Christmas tunes at the end of October
* the spirit of generosity
* my nieces patting the seat in between them at the Christmas dinner table and calling, "Sit by us, Aunt Molly"
* a big church birthday party for Jesus

May you have the greatest two gifts of all on these holidays; someone to love and someone who loves you.

JOHN SINOR

* the three kings bearing gifts
* the tick of a grandfather clock
* getting at least one gift from a relative that was knitted just for you
* gold table runners
* the town square decorated for Christmas
* angels praising God
* a twinkle in Mom and Dad's eyes
* the universal joy of Christmas
* the unshelled nut counter:
  * walnuts
  * Brazil nuts
  * peanuts
  * chestnuts
  * macadamia nuts
* the video store:
  * children's cartoons
  * Christmas specials
  * love stories
  * dramas
  * adventure movies
  * video games
* apple pie and ice cream
* the warmth of knowing that Jesus is the heart of Christmas

What are your favorite Christmas quotes and poems?

_____

_____

_____

_____

_____

_____

_____

_____

_____

_____

_____

_____

_____

_____

_____

_____

_____

_____

The earth has grown old with its burden
      of care
But at Christmas it always is young,
The heart of the jewel burns lustrous
      and fair
And its soul full of music breaks the air,
When the song of angels is sung.

PHILLIPS BROOKS

Christmas! The very word brings joy to our hearts. No matter how we may dread the rush, the long Christmas lists for gifts and cards to be bought and given—when Christmas Day comes there is still the same warm feeling we had as children, the same warmth that enfolds our hearts and our homes.

JOAN WINMILL BROWN

* the smell of new dolls
* the whimsical Christmas tree on our neighbor's roof
* the whir of the towrope
* the white lights on my Christmas tree
* golden French horns
* the whole scene before any presents are opened
* getting up before everyone else
* apricot nut bread
* the Whos down in Whoville
* the wise men's patient search
* Christmas seat cushions on the dining room chairs
* this celebration of the birth of Jesus
* thoughts while caroling
* thyme
* tin zeppelins and airplane ornaments
* Tiny Tim
* toasted garlic bread
* toddler faces peeking out of furry hoods
* the smell of pancakes and maple syrup waking you up
* Toll House cookies with walnuts
* topiary:
  * reindeer
  * bears
  * Santa and sleigh
* tossing little kids into piles of wrapping paper

✳ getting your picture taken with the mall Santa
✳ babies falling asleep with their bottles
✳ toy trains:
    ✳ wooden
    ✳ scale model
    ✳ plastic
    ✳ toddler-size ride-on trains
✳ tracing frost panes on the window
✳ Christmas socks
✳ all the different shapes, sizes and representa-
  tions of Christ's birth—the Nativity Scene. The
  reminder of what God did for us and the true
  meaning of our celebration is inspiring.
✳ Pepperidge Farm cookies

A star will come out of Jacob
*   a scepter will rise out of Israel.*

NUMBERS 24:17

I love our yearly tradition of traveling to Allegan, Michigan to ride a horse-drawn wagon around the tree farm searching for the perfect ten-foot tree. I love the smell of that freshly cut Frasier fir Christmas tree in the living room. However, it's never easy to get the tree inside the house and put it up straight and so I don't love that part!

Last year I had the new joy of watching my 16-month-old-son, Aaron, open presents! He would tear open the wrapping paper, look at the present, and say "WOW"... even though he had no idea was the gift was or what it was for!

BRIAN SCHARP

Christmas Songs and Carols

* ❋ frosty clouds of breath
* ❋ songs rising in the night
* ❋ a wood-grain guitar
* ❋ slipping and sliding on the slush
* ❋ trying to sing and laughing at the same time
* ❋ how Mom has to make sure every button and zipper on our coats is done up before we go out
* ❋ Uncle Andy's red accordion

Arise, shine, for your light has come,
*   and the glory of the LORD rises upon you.*
See, darkness covers the earth
*   and thick darkness is over the peoples,*
but the LORD rises upon you
*   and his glory appears over you.*
Nations will come to your light,
*   and kings to the brightness of your dawn.*

ISAIAH 60:1-3

❄ gold-star necklaces
❄ train tracks running under the Christmas tree
❄ tray tables
❄ tree lights that look like little candles
❄ truffles:
  ❄ mocha
  ❄ mint
  ❄ rum
  ❄ fudge
  ❄ vanilla
❄ the smell of wassail
❄ trundle beds
❄ trying out the new surfboards
❄ trying to add just one more shopping bag to the bunch you are carrying
❄ the smell of peeling an orange
❄ Uncle Dan's ice sculptures
❄ unwrapping just the end of a present to see what's inside
❄ Christmas at the Essenhaus in Middlebury, Indiana
❄ "Christmas is generous giving!"
❄ giant slush piles
❄ using cookie cutters to make Christmas cookies together
❄ vacation days from school and work

* Vail Mountain village cafés
* vanilla
* velvet party dresses
* Vick's Vaporub
* Victorian caroling costumes:
  * fur muffs
  * wool bonnets
  * lace kerchiefs
  * leather gloves
  * buttonhook boots
  * wool stockings
  * plaid scarves
  * top hats

Stars are an important part of Christmas. A special star led the wise men to Bethlehem. Jesus is called the Morning Star that rises to give light in our hearts when we believe.

At Christmas we remember that joy flows from our homes because Jesus Christ is the light we choose to follow above all others.

PAT MATUSZAK

A little child ...
A shining star,
A stable rude ...
The door ajar.
Yet in that place ...
So crude, forlorn,
The Hope of all ...
The world was born.

AUTHOR UNKNOWN

* Christmas stockings hanging over the hearth
* videotapes:
  * kids' sporting events from the past years
  * ballet and tap recitals
  * weddings
  * graduations
* the smell of walnuts when you crack their shells
* visiting family we've not seen all year
* waddling away from the table
* waking my parents on Christmas morning
* friends who share their stocking candy with me
* finding where my brothers have hidden their stocking candy from me
* "angels greet with anthems sweet"
* waking to birds chirping outside
* Waldorf salad
* walking malls with red brick pavement
* walnut-stuffed date hors d'oeurvres
* wooden figure cut-outs:
  * cats
  * ducks
  * dogs
  * farmers
  * cowboys
  * sailboats

* Christmas ties
* "raindrops on roses and whiskers on kittens"
* warm kisses in the crisp, cold air
* doing "donuts" in the car
* not even coming close to doing "donuts" in the car
* warm mittens right out of the dryer
* Christmas theme postage stamps
* "brown paper packages tied up with string"
* babysitting my brother's children so he can take his wife out for holiday dinner
* my brother babysitting for me so my husband and I can go out for holiday dinner
* my college campus decorated for the holidays
* tiptoeing outside in your socks to cut a few evergreen boughs for inside decorations
* NOT finding any spiders in the evergreen boughs you cut for inside decorations
* winning a holiday beauty pageant
* playing at a school playground in the cold
* Christmas Eve in Saltzburg, Austria
* "bright copper kettles and warm woolen mittens"

WARNING......WARNING: ADVENT VIRUS

Be on the alert for symptoms of inner Hope, Peace, Joy and Love. The hearts of a great many have already been exposed to this virus and it is possible that people everywhere could come down with it in epidemic proportions.

Some signs and symptoms of The Advent Virus:

- An unmistakable ability to enjoy each moment.
- A loss of interest in judging other people.
- A loss of interest in conflict.
- A loss of the ability to worry. (This is a very serious symptom.)
- Frequent, overwhelming episodes of appreciation.
- Contented feelings of connectedness with others and nature.
- Frequent attacks of smiling.
- An increased susceptibility to the love extended by others as well as the uncontrollable urge to extend it.

What's your favorite Christmas recipe?

_____

_____

_____

_____

_____

_____

_____

_____

_____

_____

_____

_____

_____

_____

_____

_____

_____

_____

_____

"You, Bethlehem Ephrathah,
　　　　though you are small among the clans of
　　　　　　Judah,
out of you will come for me
　　　　one who will be ruler over Israel,
whose origins are from of old,
　　　　from ancient times."

MICAH 5:2

What a blessing Christmas is! What it does for friendship! Why, if there were no Christmas, as Channing Pollock put it, we'd have to invent one, for it is the one season of the year when we can lay aside all gnawing worry, indulge in sentiment without censure, assume the carefree faith of childhood, and just plain "have fun." Whether they call it Yuletide, Noel, Weinachten, or Christmas, people around the earth thirst for its refreshment as the desert traveler for the oasis.

D. D. MONROE

* we talk about being grateful for our blessings in front of others more often at Christmas
* wearing Christmas sweatshirts to church
* the smell of roast turkey
* watching stars together
* Wedgewood serving bowls
* Bing Crosby singing "White Christmas"
* Mel Torme singing "White Christmas"
* western buckboards
* white chocolate:
  * with pecans
  * walnuts
  * coconut
  * crisped rice
* Christmas trees showing through houses' windows
* giant snowplow piles
* when Grandpa proudly shows the wooden cardholder Dad made for him as a teenager
* whispers on Christmas morning
* white as a symbol for God as Creator
* gold-trimmed goblets
* whole wheat bread
* wild turkeys in the woods

* wind chimes:
    * silver
    * bamboo
    * glass
* babies in strollers at the mall
* window quilts
* wise men and shepherds worshiping together
* wood-burning-kit name plates for the house
* "all night, all day, angels watching over me ..."

CHRISTMAS

O Father may that Holy Star
Grow every year more bright,
And send its glorious beams afar
To fill the world with light.

WILLIAM CULLEN BRYANT

AWAY IN A MANGER

Away in a manger, no crib for a bed,
The little Lord Jesus laid down His sweet head.
The stars in the sky looked down where He lay,
The little Lord Jesus, asleep on the hay.
The cattle are lowing, the Baby awakes,
But little Lord Jesus, no crying He makes;
I love Thee, Lord Jesus, look down from the sky
And stay by my cradle til morning is nigh.
Be near me, Lord Jesus, I ask Thee to stay
Close by me forever, and love me, I pray;
Bless all the dear children in Thy tender care,
And fit us for heaven to live with Thee there.

MARTIN LUTHER

Grandmother's Cinnamon Apples

These were served only at Christmas, and we kids always looked forward to this annual treat. Grandma always served them in a pretty glass bowl, and they made such a lovely addition to the table.

Peel, halve, and core 6 to 12 apples. Put them in salted water to keep them from turning brown.

Melt a four ounce package of cinnamon red hot candies in two cups of water in a saucepan over low heat. Stir until every piece of candy is melted. Decide if the color is red enough to please you and if it is not, add a few drops of red food coloring.

Rinse off the apples and put them in the cinnamon liquid. Cook gently.

Turn the apples over from time to time so they will absorb the color and liquid evenly.

Cook the apples until they are just fork tender. You don't want them to fall apart.

When finished cooking, place the apples in a pretty bowl and spoon some of the liquid over them. Chill thoroughly.

SUBMITTED BY GWEN ELLIS

* Christmas vacation
* babies learning to say, "Cookie, peese?"
* gift boxes from the orange grove
* wooden carved Santas:
  * tall skinny ones
  * round ball-like ones
  * blocks with Santa carved on them
* the smell of furniture polish: lemon or wood-scented
* woven plaid placemats
* wreaths:
  * dried flowers
  * pinecones
  * acorns
  * pine branches
  * birds' feathers
  * birds' nests
  * gold-painted walnut shells
  * bells
* miniature musical instruments
* writing a family newsletter
* yeast dough rising
* Grandfather teaching all the men in our family how to choose the perfect Christmas tree
* yellow light from each window of houses we pass at night

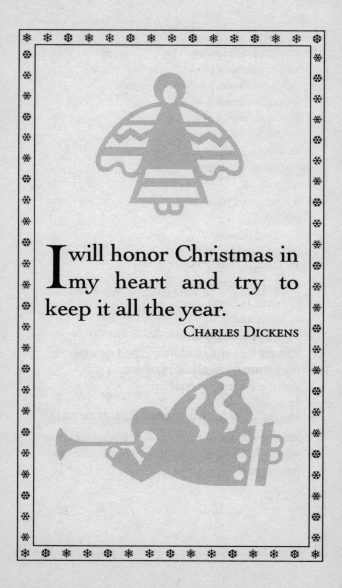

I will honor Christmas in my heart and try to keep it all the year.

CHARLES DICKENS

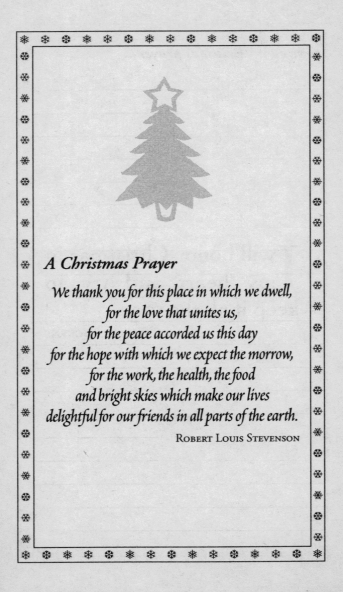

A Christmas Prayer

We thank you for this place in which we dwell,
for the love that unites us,
for the peace accorded us this day
for the hope with which we expect the morrow,
for the work, the health, the food
and bright skies which make our lives
delightful for our friends in all parts of the earth.

ROBERT LOUIS STEVENSON

Your own Christmas prayer....

❋ "a cold winter's night that was so deep"
❋ Christmas web sites
❋ gifts of gold, frankincense, and myrrh
❋ zucchini bread
❋ a pond that freezes over into a natural skating rink
❋ eating frosting right out of the can while making a Christmas cake
❋ taking a break from shopping to eat bagels and cream cheese at the bookstore coffeeshop
❋ getting stuffed animals for Christmas from your parents, even when you're 26
❋ new magic markers
❋ the green tissue paper that cushions grapefruits and oranges in those big gift boxes of fruit
❋ making bread dough ornaments and painting them with poster paints
❋ Nestor the Long-eared Donkey
❋ Avon trial-size tubes of hand lotion with Christmas art on them
❋ Winterfest at an amusement park:
  ❋ ice skating
  ❋ stage shows
  ❋ hot chocolate
  ❋ watching someone make blown-glass ornaments in the gift shop window
  ❋ riding the train around the park to look at the lights

* packing up to go home for the holidays after a long semester at college
* a chenille beret to keep your head warm
* shopping at the huge Borders store in downtown Chicago
* running into friends in the mall and stopping to show each other your purchases

The Presence of Christmas

Christmas is not just a season,
Christmas is not just a day,
Christmas is more than a reason
For parties, presents and play.
Christmas is truly the essence
Of joy that the Savior brings;
Christmas is surely the presence
Of Jesus, the Kings of Kings!

WILLIAM ARTHUR WARD

Legend of the Candy Cane

According to legend there was a candy maker in Indiana around the turn of the century who wanted to invent a candy that was a witness to Christ. The result was the candy cane.

First of all he used a hard candy because Christ is the rock of ages. This hard candy was shaped so that it would resemble either a "J" for Jesus or a shepherd's staff. He made it white to represent the purity of Christ. Finally a red stripe was added to represent the blood Christ shed for the sins of the world and three thinner red stripes for the stripes he received on our behalf when the Roman soldiers whipped him. Sometimes a green stripe is added as reminder that Jesus is a gift from God.

The flavor of the cane is peppermint which is similar to hyssop. Hyssop is in the mint family and was used in the Old Testament for purification and sacrifice. Jesus is the pure lamb of God come to be a sacrifice for the sins of the world.

So the next time you see a candy cane hear the sermon it preaches: Jesus Christ, the Good Shepherd, is the sinless rock of ages who suffered and died for our sins.

The Real Santa Claus

St. Nicholas was born in 280 AD to wealthy parents in Patera in Asia Minor. He was orphaned at a young age and became a Christian minister. St. Nicholas was elected bishop and he was once imprisoned for his faith.

Nicholas is most famous for giving. He was known to beg for food for the poor. One story claims that he would dress up in a disguise and go out into the streets and give gifts to poor children.

Some historians claim that St. Nicholas died in 343 AD, but many children believe that he is still alive giving out presents every Christmas in celebration of Christ's birth.

So remember while December
Brings the only Christmas day,
In the year let there be Christmas
In the things you do and say;
Wouldn't life be worth the living
Wouldn't dreams be coming true
If we kept the Christmas spirit
All the whole year through?

ANONYMOUS